basic

HOME STUDIO DESIGN

Printed by: MPG Books, Bodmin

Published by: Sanctuary Publishing Limited, Sanctuary House, 45-53 Sinclair Road, London
W14 0NS, United Kingdom. Web site: www.sanctuarypublishing.com

Copyright: Paul White, 2000
Sound On Sound web site: www.sospubs.co.uk

While the publishers have made every reasonable effort to trace the copyright owners for any or
all of the photographs in this book, there may be some omissions of credits for which we
apologise.

ISBN: 1-86074-272-6

basic

HOME STUDIO DESIGN

PAUL WHITE

Also by Paul White from Sanctuary Publishing

Also in this series

contents

chapter 3

chapter 4

chapter 5

chapter 6

chapter 7

chapter 8

chapter 9

introduction

It's a simple fact of music recording that both voices and instruments are affected by the acoustic environment in which they are recorded, and yet most home studios are built in rooms that were never designed with acoustics in mind. Furthermore, few home studios have the same degree of acoustic isolation as professional facilities, and so the subject of noise leaking in and out can be a serious problem.

Designers of professional recording studios allocate a large part of their budget to soundproofing and acoustic architecture, although improving the performance of a basic domestic room need not be expensive or difficult. This book aims to provide practical solutions to the more common problems of soundproofing and acoustic design that anyone with basic DIY skills can implement themselves.

soundproofing

If you're making music with a few synthesisers hooked up to a computer you can wear headphones and keep on recording even during antisocial hours, but working with acoustic instruments in the home studio can be a problem, and this can be even worse if you happen to be living in an apartment or a house that adjoins other houses, especially in modern buildings with thin walls. Most home studio operators therefore need to investigate ways of soundproofing their studios. However, it's also necessary to be realistic about what it's possible to achieve – it's seldom realistic to expect to be able to play a drum kit in a room with a wooden floor when there are other people trying to get to sleep in the room below, no matter how much money you spend on soundproofing your studio.

Soundproofing and acoustic treatment are two quite separate subjects. Acoustic treatment deals with the acoustic quality of the room from a listener's perspective, and this subject will be covered in greater detail later in the book.

no simple solution?

There is a myth that doggedly persists that sticking egg boxes to walls will soundproof a room, but this is simply not true. Although it has a marginally beneficial effect on some aspects of a room's acoustics, it has virtually no effect at all on sound leakage. There are effective practical measures that can be taken to alleviate the problem, but this isn't one of them!

The word 'soundproofing' is rather misleading, as usually the best you can hope for is to improve the situation – eliminating all sound leakage is virtually impossible, even in a room designed for the purpose. A more realistic approach is to identify how sound leakage can be reduced to the point at which it is acceptable to those outside the room. Most of the practical measures described in this book are within the scope of any practically-minded person, and nearly all of the materials are available from your local builders' merchant. However, there are some materials that must be purchased from specialist suppliers, so you may need to refer to the *Yellow Pages* or the classified ads in the back of your favourite recording magazine.

sound theory

Sound is essentially a form of energy that propagates by mechanical vibration through gases, liquids and solids. Energy cannot be destroyed, only converted to another form, so in order to 'lose' sound energy it has to be put to work that will convert it into heat energy. Sound doesn't simply continue forever for two reasons: firstly because of a law of physics called the Inverse Square Law, which dictates that sound reduces in level the further it travels from its source, simply because it is being spread out over a larger area; and secondly because it is progressively absorbed (and converted into heat) by any surfaces that it encounters and by the air that it passes through. Because it doesn't take a great deal of acoustic energy to produce a subjectively loud sound, the heating effect is negligible.

The challenge in designing effective soundproofing is to attempt to convert as much of the unwanted sound to heat as possible. The simplest way to attenuate sound is to block its path with a solid wall, and one of the most important rules to remember is that, every time the mass off a wall is doubled, the amount of sound transmitted through it is roughly halved. This means that, to cut the sound leakage through an existing wall by half, its thickness will have to be doubled.

the sound reduction index

Another important aspect of acoustic theory is the fact that the isolation provided by a structure reduces along with frequency – for every octave drop in pitch the sound isolation is halved. This is why, when you walk past a building in which loud music is playing, the bass frequencies always seem loudest. Soundproofing against high frequencies is fairly straightforward, but deep bass is very difficult to contain.

Because attenuation is dependent on a sound's frequency, the effectiveness of the sound-absorbing abilities of a partition of a particular material or design is generally measured in decibels, for a range of frequencies averaging between 100Hz to just over 3kHz, and this figure is called the SRI (Sound Reduction Index). For example, a single brick wall might have a quoted SRI of 45dB, while a wall made of the same material but twice as thick might be rated at 51dB. This is a drastic amount of attenuation, but if levels of around 100dB are produced on one side of the wall this still leaves around 50dB making it through to the other side. Also, because this is an average figure, the true leakage at the bass end will be worse.

If your studio adjoins a neighbour's house and you're separated by nothing more than a solid brick wall, it's unlikely that the degree of isolation you experience will be adequate – particularly if you monitor very loudly, play drums or have a penchant for playing slap bass through a large tube stack!

It's possible to calculate the approximate SRI of a single solid wall if you know the mass per square metre of the wall material. Of course, the final figure is dependent on the frequencies which are produced, and this number has to be factored in. This particular equation uses metric measurements to make things easier. The equation is: $R = 20 \log(fm) -47dB$, where f is the frequency of the incident sound, m is the mass of the wall (measured in kilograms per square metre) and R is the final SRI (in decibels).

However, materials that aren't completely solid behave differently from those that are, and often the only reliable way of checking the performance of a particular design is to actually measure things, as in reality the absorptive qualities of materials often vary from the figures published by the manufacturers. Furthermore, the level of isolation that can be obtained between one room and another depends on the area of the wall dividing the two rooms and on how much energy is transmitted from the wall into other parts of the structure.

Lightweight partition walls or those built out of
cinderblock will fare rather worse than those fashioned
from solid brick or concrete. For example, a light,
panelled internal door has an average SRI of around
15dB or less, and at low frequencies this is significantly
worse. However, a brick cavity wall that has been
plastered on the inside can have an average SRI of
more than 50dB.

Of course, how annoying sound leakage is depends a
great deal on the ambient noise already present in the
room on the other side. During the day, traffic noise
and other sounds will help to mask low levels of
leakage, but at night – especially out of town – even the
slightest sound will be audible. It may be unwelcome
news, but often the only practical solution is to
combine some soundproofing with a reduction in the
level of noise that you make in the first place.

air cavities

At this point, an important physical law comes into play:
if a single wall can reduce the sound leakage by 45dB or
50dB, what happens if we use two walls separated by an
air cavity? You might think (not unreasonably) that if
one wall had an SRI of 45dB, and this was placed next
to another wall with an SRI of 45dB, the result would be

a reduction in sound of 90dB, which would be terrific. However, it isn't quite that simple; unless the walls are separated by a considerable gap, the air between them carries energy and reduces the efficiency of the isolation. The wider the gap, the better the isolation.

Isolation barriers based on the construction of multiple walls separated by air cavities tend to be the most successful in reducing sound leakage, and a double structure will invariably perform significantly better than a single-layer barrier of similar mass, and the overall isolation improves if the air cavity is wider. Methods of constructing such walls will be covered later in this book, but there are much weaker areas than walls that need to be tackled first.

problem areas

It's no good trying to improve walls if the doors and windows leak like sieves. Even double-glazed windows offer a much more limited amount of sound isolation when compared with a solid wall, although they are still significantly better than single-glazed windows. You may be able to make improvements in this area yourself by implementing extra internal glazing with a large air cavity and heavy glass, or if you don't need the light at all you could fill the window space with sandbags and board it up. Heavy curtains help a little, but they don't make a great deal of difference, especially at low frequencies. Remember: even the smallest gap can leak a lot of sound, so everything needs to be quite airtight.

If you have a window that you don't need to open, you can make it airtight very quickly by using a gun to apply mastic sealant to the frame, which is effective and not too difficult to peel off when you need to open the window. Doors need to be opened continually, however, and it's surprising exactly how much sound leaks through and around most internal doors. Because of the light construction of modern interior doors, significant improvements can be made by fitting good seals and increasing the door's mass, either by replacing it with a heavier one or by shoring up both sides with extra bulk. However, even the heaviest single door will leak significantly more sound than a double door with an air cavity between. If you're serious in soundproofing your studio, you must prepare yourself for the eventuality that you may have to fit two doors to each opening.

floors and ceilings

You'll be glad to hear that concrete floors actually help to improve sound isolation because of their mass, but unfortunately wooden floors can be a real problem.

Even if you build a floating floor above the original structure, the leakage will still be worse than that through a solid brick wall, and it's very difficult to get rid of boomy resonances. Without major structural work, it's very unlikely that you'll be able to use a drum kit in a room with a wooden floor without disturbing whoever is below you, and few domestic rooms or apartments have high enough ceilings to accommodate a full floating floor. Don't move quite yet, though, because in some situations a degree of noise leakage may be acceptable, and there are also strategies that can be employed to noticeably improve the situation without the need for too much structural upheaval.

If floors are difficult, ceilings are ten times worse. Whatever soundproofing material you add, you're going to have to find some way of holding it up there, whereas with floors gravity is on your side. There's not a lot that can be done to make dramatic improvements, short of building a substantial false ceiling below the original, but a couple of layers of thick underfelt below the carpet in the room above can improve things considerably. You can also treat the original ceiling.

To illustrate just how difficult the problem can be, a professional studio usually has a completely separate inner room built inside the existing room, isolated from the original floor by blocks of neoprene rubber. Most home studios simply don't have the space to do this, let alone the money, but if you're in a position to try it, the basics of room-within-a-room construction will be covered later in the book. A further advantage of this design is that the addition of any further acoustic treatment is often very simple because, as the studio is built around a properly-designed inner shell, the acoustics are more predictable.

overview

The laws of physics are most definitely not on your side when it comes to keeping sound in or out. Don't let that discourage you, though, as the simplest and least expensive treatments often produce the greatest improvements (sealing gaps around windows and doors, adding double glazing and so on).

By taking a common-sense approach to implementing the principles outlined in this book, you should be able to make noticeable improvements at a minimal cost. Before you do anything, however, you should first check out the walls, floors, ceilings, windows and doors in the studio to identify those places where the worst leakage occurs, so that you can concentrate your resources on the weak areas. Sound will leak out even if the room has just one ill-fitting door or window, rendering the rest of your efforts pointless.

For soundproofing at its most basic, you will need to have considerable structural mass and airtight seals added to doors and windows, but you'll also need to consider sound that's actually communicated by structures and find ways to avoid it. This is important, because sound travels very efficiently as mechanical vibrations through solid structures, such as wooden joists or steel girders. There's little point in getting everything else right if your soundproofing is rendered ineffective by an ill-considered structural feature.

coming up for air

A soundproofed room is an airtight room, so it's also important to consider how to ventilate a studio. Is it enough just to open doors between takes, or is it necessary to install an air-conditioning system? Simple air conditioners do nothing more than cool and recirculate the air already present in the room, but air conditioners designed for professional studios pipe in fresh air from outside, and these need silencer baffles, large ducting, anti-vibration mountings and so on. This is likely to cost more than most complete home studios, so the usual compromise is to fit a recirculating air conditioner (cooler) and occasionally open the doors.

pragmatism

Major construction or alteration is out of the question for most home studio owners, who usually have to rely on upgrading what already exists. You may also need to compromise on the amount of noise you make. If you can't reduce the amount of noise as much as you'd like by soundproofing your studio, you may have to find a compromise that keeps all parties happy.

sound leakage

Sound isolation can be significantly improved with simple DIY techniques, but you shouldn't expect miracles. What you can expect, however, is a useful reduction in the level of sound leaking into and out of your studio, and in a typical home studio most of this noise escapes through floors, ceilings, windows and doors. Lightweight partition walls are also less than ideal as sound isolators, although those walls that have been properly constructed or upgraded can be reasonably effective.

Ceilings and wooden floors tend to be weak spots when it comes to sound isolation, because they are significantly less massive than the walls of an average room. If you're on a budget, perhaps the most effective measure you can employ when dealing with floors is to fit thick hair to the floor of the studio and, if possible, also beneath the carpet in the room above. The weight and thickness of the combined carpet and underfelt provides both absorption and damping, so it's important to buy the heaviest grade possible. Foam underlay isn't nearly as good as the matted felt type in preventing sound leakage.

However, the greatest improvement can usually be made by uprating doors and windows, so these will be tackled first. If your studio isn't equipped with double-glazed windows, your windows will almost certainly be the biggest cause of sound leakage. That said, even double-glazed units are of only limited use, and will leak a considerably greater amount of sound than the surrounding walls. For this reason, the fitting of additional internal glazing behind the original windows is strongly recommended. If you're working in a room with regular single-glazed windows, however, secondary double-glazing should be considered absolutely essential, unless you're prepared to block up the window aperture altogether with a shutter or sandbags. The secondary double glazing which can be purchased in DIY stores is reasonably cost effective, and because the space between the original window and the secondary glazing is usually quite large in comparison with that between panes of a regular double-glazed window you'll probably find that the amount of sound reduction is actually rather better. It also helps to use the thickest glass you can find for the internal glazing, as more mass translates into less leakage, especially at lower frequencies.

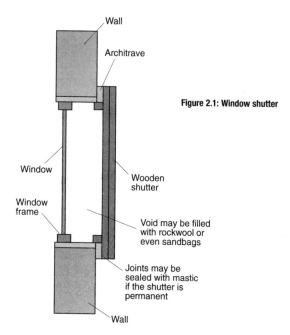

Figure 2.1: Window shutter

window shutters

If you're prepared to forego the luxury of daylight, the cheap and cheerful solution is to block off the window with a heavy shutter, made from either wood or MDF (a high-density fibreboard), which can be screwed over the window opening as demonstrated in Figure 2.1.

Thumbscrew sash window fasteners can be fitted if the shutter has to be taken down between sessions, but if it can be kept in place then matters can be improved further by stuffing the void between the window and the shutter with mineral wool insulation, which will damp any resonances in the panel and the window glass. Any gaps can be sealed with acrylic frame sealant, applied with a mastic gun, while heavy curtains will also help a little. Sandbags are effective at isolating sound, but they're also very heavy, so it's important to ensure that they're properly supported. It's also important that the sand is perfectly dry before the bags are filled.

doors

A typical lightweight internal door, with plywood skins and a cardboard honeycomb filling, probably provides around 15dB of isolation at best, and much less than this at low frequencies. This figure shrinks if there's a gap under or around the door, so a heavier door should be fitted at the very least. Don't try to upgrade the existing door, though, as it probably won't be strong enough to hold the additional layers.

Even the heaviest door will provide a much smaller amount of sound attenuation than that provided by a

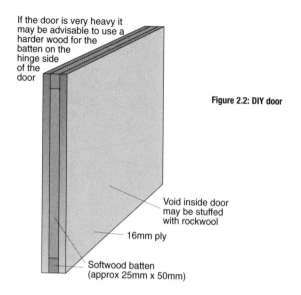

If the door is very heavy it may be advisable to use a harder wood for the batten on the hinge side of the door

Figure 2.2: DIY door

Void inside door may be stuffed with rockwool

16mm ply

Softwood batten (approx 25mm x 50mm)

solid wall, but you should be able to improve significantly on 15dB! Gluing and screwing a layer of three-quarter-inch (20mm) plywood onto a solid timber door is one effective measure that can be taken, but only if the door makes a virtually airtight seal with the frame.

If it's your intention to build your own doors from two layers of thick-ply MDF or chipboard, leaving a gap between the two layers of ply and stuffing the remaining space with mineral wool or fibreglass will help to deaden any vibration of the panels and will also absorb a proportion of the sound radiating from one panel to the other. Because chipboard isn't a structurally resilient material, the hinges must be supported with hardwood inserts. Plywood is a much stronger material, however, and although it's more expensive it makes the job a lot easier. Figure 2.2 shows the general principles behind the construction of a door.

It's important to make sure that all doors in your studio are as airtight as possible, and to achieve this heavy-duty seals should be fitted around the edges, not forgetting the threshold between the door and the floor. A compression latch may also be fitted, similar to those on industrial freezers, so that the door is squeezed shut more tightly as the handle is pulled down. These latches are mechanically simple devices – a tapered plastic wedge is screwed to the doorframe so that the door is forced harder against the seal as the handle is closed.

Figure 2.3 shows how door seals are fitted. The simplest type is a foam neoprene strip with a semi-circular cross section, which can be stuck in place with contact adhesive. Most suppliers of studio

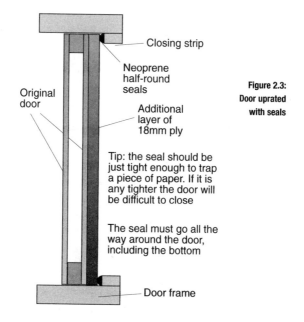

Closing strip

Neoprene
half-round
seals

Original
door

Additional
layer of
18mm ply

**Figure 2.3:
Door uprated
with seals**

Tip: the seal should be
just tight enough to trap
a piece of paper. If it is
any tighter the door will
be difficult to close

The seal must go all the
way around the door,
including the bottom

Door frame

materials will be able to find these components,
including the seal material.

The simplest way to fit the seals correctly is first to hang
the door in the frame and then glue the seals to the
wooden closing strips before nailing them in place. With
the door closed, the strips can then be pinned in place

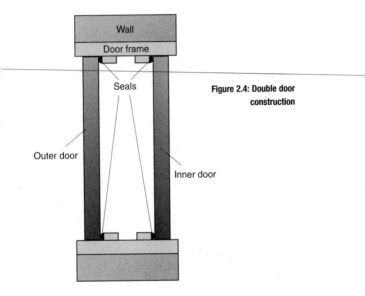

Figure 2.4: Double door construction

one at a time so that the seal is just touching the surface of the door. (If you try to make the seal compress more than a tiny amount you'll have great difficulty in closing the door again, especially if you don't have a compression latch.) The seals should be fitted just tight enough to grip a thin piece of paper when the door is closed. The closing strips can then be screwed permanently in place, once you're sure that the door is fitting correctly – and that you can close it properly!

double doors

No matter what improvements you make to a single door, in those situations where a lot of isolation is needed the law of diminishing returns makes it much more effective to fit a double door. In most rooms it's possible to fit doors to both sides of a wall, leaving a gap the thickness of the walls between them, as shown in Figure 2.4. Both doors should be fitted with seals, but only one of these needs to have a pressure latch; the outer door can have a spring closer or a conventional latch. The inside of the doorframes in professional studios may be equipped with elaborate sound traps, but for most DIY purposes it should be enough just to stick a one-inch layer of fireproof furniture foam around the inside of the space between the doors.

If at all possible, when constructing a double door it's best to use two separate doorframes rather than a single wide frame, as this will help to prevent sound vibrations from travelling from the first door to the second door across the doorframe. In commercial studios, frames are often isolated from the surrounding brickwork by a layer of neoprene sheeting. This might be a little extreme for a home studio, but if you're building a studio from scratch or converting a garage it may prove worthwhile, while gaps may be filled with expanding foam filler or mastic. In an existing doorway, the original doorframe can be used.

patio doors

Commercial patio doors provide a convenient means of dividing the performing area of the studio and control room because they double as both a viewing window and a door. However, in order to achieve adequate sound isolation, two sets of double-glazed patio doors should be used, with a gap between them of at least nine inches in order to provide a reasonable amount of low-frequency isolation. A larger gap also helps compensate for any deficiencies in the door seals.

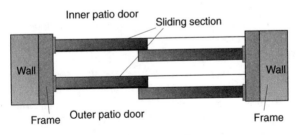

The wider the gap between the two patio doors, the better the sound isolation

Figure 2.5: Double patio doors

The walls within the cavity formed by the two sets of doors should be lined with acoustic foam. Figure 2.5 shows a practical way of using patio doors to divide live and recording areas.

summary

- Doors in a studio must be as heavy as possible, as well as airtight. A double-door assembly will always outperform a single door in attenuating sound levels.

- Sound travels well through solid materials, so neoprene sheeting can be used to isolate structures such as doorframes, studding wall frames and suchlike from the main structure.

- Mineral wool stuffed into air cavities will help to provide both absorption and damping, while aerosol polyurethane foam is useful for filling small gaps. Mastic or frame sealant can be used for filling smaller gaps.

- For windows, double or triple glazing is invariably the best answer, unless you can afford to block the windows entirely. In any event, the window frames must be airtight.

- For the most effective isolation, when new windows are installed the glass panes should be isolated from their respective frames with neoprene or foam rubber glass mounting strips.

- At low frequencies, the effect of mass, combined with air cavities, forms the only really effective barrier.

walls, floors and ceilings

Fixing problems with the windows and doors should stop most sound from escaping, but thin walls, floors, ceilings or even walls may be too light to offer a useful amount of sound isolation, which means you'll also need to attend to these.

If you're lucky, your studio will have solid walls, but if you want to build a partition wall to separate the control room from your studio you'll need to line this new wall with extra layers of plasterboard in order to make it sufficiently massive to block enough sound. If your studio has a solid floor you should really forget the lightweight wall and use concrete blocks, but if you must use a partition wall (if the room has a wooden floor, for example) it's important to include an air cavity, as well as making it as heavy as possible – lightweight studding walls don't have enough mass to act as effective sound isolators, especially at low frequencies, even though they often comprise two layers separated by an air cavity.

If you have plenty of space and you're starting from scratch, the best thing to do is build two separate studding walls, as you can separate these with a relatively large air cavity; but if you don't want to cut down on the size of the room, a simple four-inch-thick frame lined with several layers of plasterboard on both sides can also be quite effective, although this kind of wall has to be fixed in place carefully because sound energy travels quite happily within solids. The frame must also be isolated from the rest of the structure so that vibrations aren't transmitted either to or from the floor, walls or ceiling. Unfortunately, this isolation can never be perfect, as the frame will need something on which to rest, but if a resilient material is used – such as neoprene – the improvement will be worthwhile.

Quarter-inch neoprene rubber sheeting or dense neoprene foam between the frame and the floor is very effective, and this should also be used at those points where the wall touches other walls and the ceiling. Alternatively, a thick rubber car mat cut into strips can also be used. Some energy leakage is inevitable, as the fixing screws transmit vibrations, but this shouldn't be too disastrous.

Once the frame has been constructed, it must be

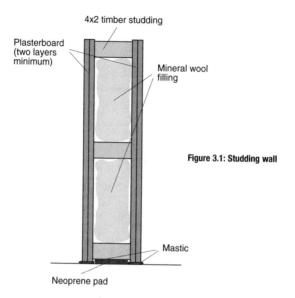

4x2 timber studding

Plasterboard
(two layers
minimum)

Mineral wool
filling

Figure 3.1: Studding wall

Mastic

Neoprene pad

panelled on both sides with at least two layers of
plasterboard, and the thicker 12mm grade should be
used if possible in order to keep the mass as high as
possible. The boards must also be staggered so that the
seams don't coincide, and temporary spacers made
from hardboard or wood off-cuts should be used to
make sure that the plasterboard stops just short of
touching the existing walls, floor or ceiling. The
insertion of a layer of lightweight fibreboard between

the two layers of plasterboard can also improve the damping of the wall without adding too much to its mass, and plastering the surface on completion will also help. However, if at all possible the space around the edge should be sealed with mastic rather than filled with plaster. Figure 3.1 demonstrates the construction of a studding wall.

double studding walls

Although they are quite simple to build, basic studding walls can be quite ineffective because their frames can conduct vibrational energy from one surface to the other. This can be ameliorated by nailing the plasterboard to the frame while separating them with rubber or felt spacers, but perhaps the best approach is to build a double frame structure, as shown in Figure 3.2. Here the timbers are staggered to fit between each other so that the wall isn't that much thicker than it already was. In either case, if the void between the two sides of the wall is stuffed with mineral wool loft insulation, this will help absorb any energy trying to pass through the void, and it will also reduce problems with resonance. These diagrams only show the timber fitted in one direction, but in practice studding walls comprise both vertical studs and horizontal noggins.

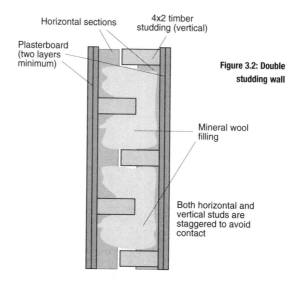

Horizontal sections

4x2 timber
studding (vertical)

Plasterboard
(two layers
minimum)

**Figure 3.2: Double
studding wall**

Mineral wool
filling

Both horizontal and
vertical studs are
staggered to avoid
contact

uprating an existing wall

You may be in a situation where an existing wall
doesn't provide enough isolation, either because it's
too thin or because it's fashioned from a lightweight
building material, such as cinderblock. Such walls can
be lined with studding and plasterboard by using
similar constructional techniques to those used in
building freestanding studding walls – as previously
described – except only one side of the frame needs to

be covered. Ideally, there should be a small gap between the frame and the existing wall – which is again best achieved by using neoprene spacers – although screwing the studding to the wall and separating them with compressed mineral wool is also effective. (The cavity can be filled with mineral wool before the plasterboard skin is nailed in place.)

Again, two or more layers of plasterboard are required to build up enough mass, and it also helps to insert a layer of fibreboard in the middle, as layering with different materials creates an acoustic mismatch, reducing the amount of vibrational energy which is transmitted and damping out resonances. Figure 3.3 shows an existing wall being upgraded by the addition of a studding/plasterboard layer.

When constructing walls where two or more layers of board are being used, it's often a good idea to seal the gaps between boards with flexible mastic or frame sealant before fixing the next layer. It's also helpful to use dabs of plasterboard adhesive between adjacent layers of plasterboard, which will prevent the panels from resonating independently, and if you have the space to add even more layers of plasterboard then so much the better, as long as your existing wall and floor can take the weight.

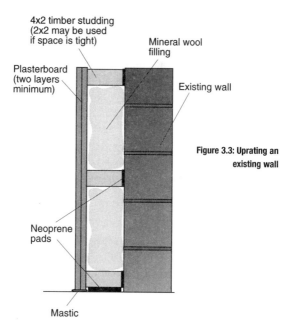

4x2 timber studding
(2x2 may be used
if space is tight)

Mineral wool
filling

Plasterboard
(two layers
minimum)

Existing wall

Figure 3.3: Uprating an
existing wall

Neoprene
pads

Mastic

Unless many layers of plasterboard are used to create a
very heavy wall, the attenuation at low frequencies will
probably be less than that offered by a solid brick or
concrete wall. Even so, the improvement should still
be worthwhile. If it proves necessary to build an
internal wall, you should check the ratio of the height,
width and length of your newly-created rooms to see if

41

you might be inviting problems with acoustics. As a rule, the worst possible situation is having equal dimensions for width, height and depth, as the room will resonate powerfully at specific frequencies. For this reason, it's also important to avoid the situation where one dimension is an exact multiple of either of the other two – the ratios should be kept as random as possible. Don't panic if the ratios of your room are less than ideal, though, because most problems can be avoided by using sensibly-chosen near-field monitors.

floors

If you have a concrete floor then you're probably starting from a reasonably good position, but if your studio is in a bedroom with a wooden floor then you're going to run into problems. A typical domestic floor is a relatively poor sound isolator, and most noisy equipment – not to mention tapping feet – will be in direct contact with the floor, which will makes things worse. It's therefore necessary to tackle structurally-borne sound, and the cheapest first step is to fit heavy felt underlay beneath the studio carpet. Once this has been done, any noisy equipment must removed from contact with the floor – monitors should be placed on speaker stands and fixed in place with blobs of Blu Tac, and guitar amps should be placed on blocks of thick foam rubber.

Drum kits are even more problematic, and it's unrealistic to expect the amateur DIY enthusiast to be able to provide anything like complete isolation. The most effective way to insulate a drum kit is to construct a shallow plinth or raft on which to set up the kit and isolate this from the floor by standing it on thick foam rubber. If this fails to provide adequate isolation, the next step is to consider building what's know as a floating floor.

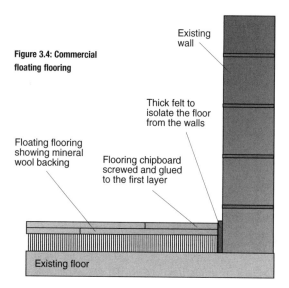

Figure 3.4: Commercial floating flooring

Existing wall

Thick felt to isolate the floor from the walls

Floating flooring showing mineral wool backing

Flooring chipboard screwed and glued to the first layer

Existing floor

floating floors

A floating floor is simply a false floor mounted on acoustic isolators above your existing floor. It must have resilient material around the edge so that it doesn't come into direct contact with the walls, but it doesn't need to be more than a few inches deep, so you don't have to lose much in the way of ceiling height.

Most lightweight floating floors are built with studding-and flooring-grade chipboard, but specially-made material can be bought which comprises chipboard with mineral wool bonded to the underside. This type of structure won't be too heavy for most domestic floors to support, and it won't be too difficult to lay onto the existing floor surface. Once the floor is down, a second layer of flooring chipboard should then be glued and screwed to the first layer, with the joints staggered. This lends strength and rigidity to the floor, and also prevents the individual panels from drifting apart. Figure 3.4 shows a floating floor construction based on a commercial flooring board with a mineral wool backing.

The same type of flooring may also be used as a foundation on which to build a small room-within-a-room type of studio, with studding or plasterboard walls, as long as the weight of the inner room isn't great

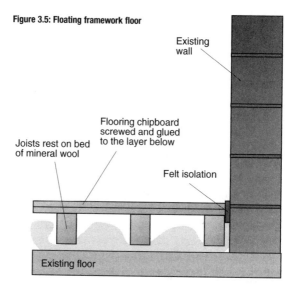

Figure 3.5: Floating framework floor

Existing wall

Flooring chipboard screwed and glued to the layer below

Joists rest on bed of mineral wool

Felt isolation

Existing floor

enough to cause the floor to bow under its weight. However, the preferred DIY option is to construct the inner room so that its walls are supported by neoprene isolators resting directly on the original flooring. In this method of construction, the floating floor is a non-load-bearing surface. While building a room within a room isn't usually an option in a studio in your average bedroom, it may be a practical option if you're converting a large garage or building a separate studio.

An alternative to using the conventional floating flooring material currently commercially available is to build a two-by-two-inch or two-by-four-inch wooden frame and cover it with two layers of flooring chipboard. This may then be separated from the original floor by blocks of neoprene, although the most common approach is simply to cover the existing floor with mineral wool loft insulation and then place the studding raft on top of that. Follow the guidelines concerning sound isolation outlined in the previous chapter by not allowing the floor to touch the existing walls at any point and filling any gaps with mastic or silicone rubber to ensure that the floor is airtight. (Figure 3.5 shows a studding floor.)

ceilings

When soundproofing a ceiling, you're plagued with all of the problems associated with soundproofing a floor, but you don't have gravity on your side, helping you to keep your sound isolation treatments in place. Acoustic foam tiles are light, but they keep out very little sound. The sandbags and lead sheeting used in commercial designs are obviously not an option, so your first step should be to fit underfelt to the room above your studio. If it belongs to someone else, you could offer to pay to have it fitted.

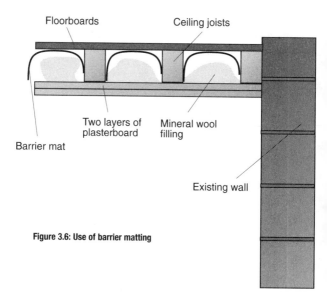

Figure 3.6: Use of barrier matting

If you're serious about taking things even further, it's important to find out if the floor above is made from floorboards or chipboard. Chipboard floors are reasonably airtight, but floorboards may well have gaps between them, in which case you'll need to remove the ceiling plaster or plasterboard to expose the joists, which will give you access to the undersides of the floorboards of the room above. You should start by filling in all of the gaps with mastic, but to do the job properly you should also fit barrier matting between the joists, as shown in Figure 3.6. Barrier matting is a heavy, flexible material that has many uses in studio construction, but you'll probably only be able to obtain it from a supplier of studio materials. It's constructed with a mineral-loaded plastic, and looks rather like a black, flexible linoleum, but is in fact much heavier. It can be fixed in place by using a powered staple gun or with flat-headed roofing nails, but you'll need somebody to help you take the weight until you've got enough staples in place to hold up the material.

Once the barrier matting is in place, the gaps between the joists can be stuffed with mineral wool loft insulation and the underside of the joists covered with at least two layers of 12mm plasterboard. Hire a plasterer to skim the plasterboard and you'll have a smooth new ceiling, as well as reduced sound leakage.

suspended ceilings

It can also help to fit a false ceiling, if you have height to spare, but if you don't know exactly what you're doing you should employ a professional builder, because the size of the joists you will need will depend on the length they are required to span. The approach behind fitting a false ceiling is shown in Figure 3.7. Before you start,

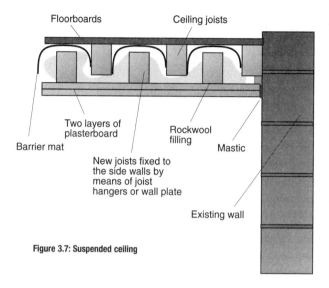

Figure 3.7: Suspended ceiling

however, the old ceiling still has to be stripped of plasterboard and treated in the same way as the previous example. Notice also that the joists for the new ceiling are fixed between the existing ceiling joists to minimise any loss in height, although if you have plenty of headroom to play with you can simply leave the original ceiling as it was and build the new one beneath it. The void between the original ceiling and the suspended ceiling should again be stuffed with mineral wool, in order to prevent resonance.

A suspended ceiling is built from joists and plasterboard in much the same way as a studding partition wall, and is supported by wooden wall plates, which are fixed to the original walls, so the original walls must be of solid construction. Again, isolation is better with more massive false ceilings, but a layer of lightweight insulation board can be introduced between the plasterboard layers without incurring much of a weight penalty. If you're considering putting up more than two layers of plasterboard, you should employ the services of a builder or architect to check that the existing ceiling will support the additional weight.

chapter 4

rooms within rooms

If you have enough space and a large enough budget, the ideal way to build a studio is to start off with a large, solid-walled building and then construct additional rooms inside. These inner rooms should be self-contained structures, equipped with floating floors, and shouldn't be in physical contact with the main shell of the building other than via neoprene isolation blocks. Low-frequency isolation is more effective if there is a large gap between the inner room and the outer shell, and a gap of eight inches should be considered the minimum.

Building one room inside another creates a double-walled construction with a large air cavity, and also eliminates most sources of structurally-borne sound by isolating the inner room from the outer shell. The degree of isolation that can be achieved depends largely on the type and construction of the floating floor and the studio walls. As a rule, the more massive the floating floor, and the greater the space between it and the true floor below, the more effective it will be at blocking

**Figure 4.1: Alternative
wall construction**

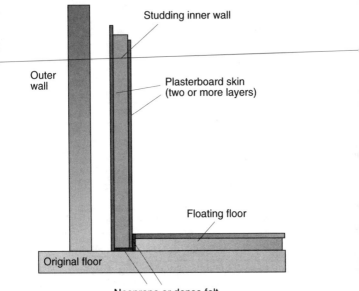

Studding inner wall

Outer
wall

Plasterboard skin
(two or more layers)

Floating floor

Original floor

Neoprene or dense felt

sounds at low frequencies (although in smaller, private studios the type of floating floor discussed in the previous chapter is usually adequate).

For those interested in the mechanics of construction, the inner room can be thought of as a mass supported by a spring, and the degree of isolation which can be achieved can be extremely high if the resonant frequency of this mass/spring system is lower than the lowest sound frequencies being generated.

a practical solution

For smaller studios, it's often adequate to construct a relatively lightweight inner room, as long as it follows the same general principles as the double-skinned studding wall described earlier. The timber framework for the walls is made by building planks of four-by-two-inch timber directly onto the existing floor via neoprene isolation strips, while the ceiling joists are fixed to the wall frames. Ceiling joists may need to be two inches by six inches deep or more, depending on the span which needs to be covered, but unless the room is fairly small you should really consult an architect or an experienced builder to help you with the constructional details before starting work. Figure 4.1 shows this type of construction. You should also consult an architect if the underlying floor isn't solid, in order to determine whether the floor will safely support the inner room.

doors

Doorways are obvious weak spots, as far as sound isolation is concerned, and a double-door construction

Figure 4.2: Fitting a door

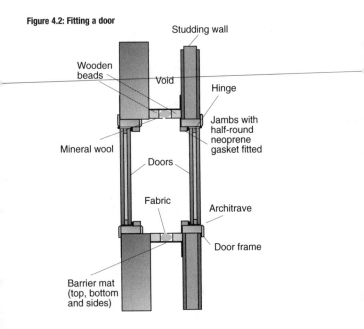

(one door in the inner room and one in the outer shell) is essential in order to maintain the isolation of a room within a room. It's also advisable to use barrier matting, which will help to isolate the space between the doors from the void between the inner and outer rooms, and Figure 4.2 shows how this may be achieved. At least one of the doors should be fitted with compression latches, and proper door seals should be fitted to both doors.

Figure 4.3: Fitting a window

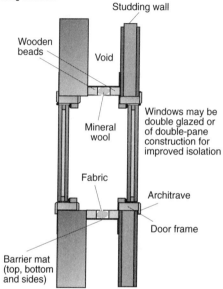

Also, sound isolation is more effective with doors of a heavier construction. Similar precautions should also be taken when building windows – the inner and outer frames may be positioned close to each other, but it's essential that there is some gap between them in order to prevent vibrations from being transmitted from the inner shell to the outer wall. Figure 4.3 shows a practical way of arranging this.

double rooms

Where two inner rooms are built inside the same outer room, sound leaking from one room to the other can be a problem. This can be improved by using an airtight curtain of barrier matting between the rooms, which will provide a degree of isolation between the void surrounding one inner room and the void around the other. Alternatively, barrier matting may be used to seal off the void at the point at which the two rooms meet, as shown in Figure 4.4.

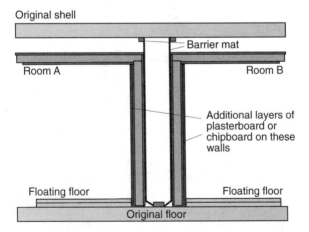

Figure 4.4: Inter-room isolation

acoustic treatment

Soundproofing relies on principles that are fairly straightforward, but acoustic design is often seen as being something of a black art. A good listening room should sound neither too live nor too dead, and to achieve this it's usual to combine the use of sound-absorbing materials with the practise of distributing surfaces in a way that breaks up strong reflections. How this is done depends on the amount of money available (professional studio designers go to great lengths to create the best possible listening environments), but huge improvements can be made in the smaller studio both simply and cheaply, without having to resort to advanced mathematics.

practicalities

Even if you understand the complex maths needed to calculate the acoustic behaviour of a particular room, accurately treating the room's acoustics is not a process that can be undertaken purely based on theory, because the equations are notoriously imprecise for small rooms and the building materials involved may not have the acoustic properties that are stated in the materials catalogues. Furthermore, the acoustic properties of a room depend to a large extent on its contents.

Professional studio designers use a combination of maths, measurement and experience to arrive at a satisfactory solution, and the measuring equipment they use (which tends to be expensive) requires specialised knowledge in order to be operated. Don't worry, though – this isn't the only method; fortunately it's possible to improve a listening space significantly by applying a few basic rules. What's more, because home recording tends to rely heavily on near-field monitors, the contribution of a room's acoustic isn't as significant as it would be in a larger room, where monitors would be positioned further away from the listener.

The trick is to improve the room by doing as little to it as possible. Fortunately, a domestic room that's carpeted and equipped with just a few items of furniture is already pretty close to being an acceptable listening environment. The purpose of this chapter is to examine some of the basic principles of acoustics so that home studio enthusiasts will know what they're dealing with, and will hopefully also be dissuaded from doing anything that might make the situation worse.

For example, it has been known for people to carpet the entire wall area of their studios – usually with disastrous results.

the studio area

A control room needs to provide the best possible environment in which to listen to and evaluate the music being recorded and mixed. The performing area of the studio, on the other hand, doesn't have to be accurate; it just needs to sound good. For example, some studios have stone and wooden live rooms, rooms with variable acoustics, neutral rooms and, occasionally, fairly dead rooms – all of which can be appropriate environments for the recording of certain kinds of music. Invariably, a compromise has to be sought in the home studio, where the recording and mixing is carried out in the same room.

dead acoustics

A relatively dead recording environment excludes nearly all natural room ambience, enabling the engineer to start with a clean slate when it comes to adding artificial effects. Most leading engineers and producers would agree that instruments which require a live acoustic setting invariably sound better in a sympathetic live room than when processed with artificial ambience from a digital reverb unit or echo plate, but it's probably fair to say that a reasonably dead room is more useful than a very live one if it's the only room you have.

live acoustics

Separate live rooms are always popular for the recording of drums or certain other acoustic instruments, and a typical live room might consist of an untreated stone or tiled room with an exposed concrete or wooden floor. It's possible to create a more general-purpose recording area (if there's enough room) by creating an area that's live at one end but damped at the other. Acoustic screens that are reflective on one side and absorbent on the other may then be used to create localised areas which have the desired acoustic characteristic, and also provide some separation between instruments. Moveable carpets or heavy drapes may also be used to deaden a naturally live room.

control rooms

While studio acoustics may vary, depending on the type of music which is being recorded, the control room must provide a control environment in which recordings may be evaluated and in which valid musical decisions can be taken. However, because of the multiplicity of different monitor speaker systems and the widely differing designs of control rooms, the aim of creating anything approaching a universal standard has yet to be realised. Most acoustic designers agree in broad terms to what constitutes a good listening room, but few professional studios sound exactly alike.

reflections

Why should a room have a sound at all when you're really listening to the speakers? In reality, sound reflects from all solid surfaces, and so when a sound source (such as a loudspeaker) stops producing sound, the reflections continue for a short period of time until the energy is absorbed. In effect, the room functions as an energy store, returning some of the acoustic energy to the air some time after the initial event.

Because of the presence of these reflections, as well as hearing the direct sound from our monitor loudspeakers, we also hear an appreciable amount of reverberation, which is produced as the sound bounces around the room. In a good listening room, the reverb time will be too short to be perceptible under normal circumstances (although you'd notice if it were absent altogether). However, different materials and structures reflect different parts of the audio spectrum more than others, and the dimensions of the room cause resonances or modes to be set up, so the reflected or indirect sound we hear is coloured (ie it doesn't have a flat frequency response).

The ideal listening room needs a touch of reverb to help increase the perceived loudness of the monitors, and also to prevent the room from sounding unnaturally dead. On the other hand, the reverb time also needs to be roughly equal at all frequencies across the audio spectrum if coloration is to be avoided. Reverb times of between 0.2 and 0.4 seconds are normally chosen for control rooms, although it's also common for the reverb time of very low frequencies to be slightly longer – except in very sophisticated studios, where elaborate bass-trapping techniques are used.

An even reverberation time can only be achieved by the careful deployment of different types of sound-absorbing or sound-scattering materials and structures. Formulae exist that make it possible to calculate the areas of treatment, but relying purely on calculations is likely to lead to inaccurate results – not only because the formulae work best for large spaces but also because variables in the performance of the materials will throw out the figure. If you add the effect of reflective and resonant studio equipment introduced after the design's completion, along with the presence of other people in the studio, it's clear why it's virtually impossible to predict the acoustics of a room accurately.

It's also likely that the existing building has acoustic properties that can't be calculated accurately. Because of this, professional studio designers use very sophisticated measuring equipment to check the room's acoustics both before and after treating the room, not just simple spectrum analysers.

control room compromises

Most home studio recording is carried out in the control room rather than in the studio itself, so the design of the control room may end up being a compromise between ergonomics and acoustics, especially when equipment is regularly being moved in and out. Even when the performance of the room has been brought within acceptable parameters, the choice and location of loudspeakers can still have a dramatic effect on the overall monitoring accuracy of the room, and this subject will be covered later in the book.

modes

All rooms suffer from reflections and resonances. The frequencies at which a room resonates depends on its internal dimensions, and every room exhibits modes, which cause the spectrum of the reflected sound to fluctuate at different points within the room. In rooms which have solid walls, the modes which are then produced are directly related to that room's particular dimensions.

If a sound wave is generated that has exactly the same wavelength as the longest dimension of a room, it will be reflected back and forth from the facing walls in phase with the original, thus reinforcing it, creating a phenomenon known as a standing wave. For example, with the speed of sound being roughly 1,100 feet per second, an eleven-feet-long room would thus correspond to a half wavelength at 50Hz, the result being a mode or resonance of 50Hz.

Any sound reproduced in the room would therefore undergo an artificial reinforcement or coloration of sounds at or around 50Hz and its multiples. Two half wavelengths at 100Hz also fit neatly into eleven feet, three at 150Hz, four at 200Hz, and so on. Introducing sound into the room at any of these frequencies will cause standing waves, giving rise to potential trouble spots at every increase in frequency of 50Hz.

However, this is only in relation to one room dimension. The width and height of a room also give rise to their own series of standing-wave frequencies. Because they're related to the three axes of the room (length, width and height), modes caused by standing waves between parallel room surfaces are known as axial modes.

There are other, more complex modes that cause problems in the studio, which are produced by sound bouncing off more than one wall and travelling around the room, and these are known as tangential and oblique modes. Because these modes are produced by sounds bouncing off more surfaces, some energy is absorbed or scattered, and so the intensity of the modal peaks is less than it is for axial modes. (Tangential modes produce half the energy of axial modes, whereas oblique modes produce a quarter of the energy of the axial modes.) These modes decay at different rates, and so absorbing material must be placed in an area of high pressure in order to damp a mode. For example, to damp a mode produced by two opposite walls, the absorbent material must be placed on one of the walls, rather than on the floor or on the ceiling.

optimum dimensions

Modes will continue to exist unless at least one of every opposing pair of surfaces is made to be completely absorbent across the entire audio spectrum, although the absorbency of the walls will influence the intensity of these modes. The problem is: how can these resonances be reconciled with a flat reverb spectrum?

It turns out that, if the modes are fairly evenly distributed and not too widely spaced, there should be no drastic peaks or dips in a room's frequency response. In practice, modal problems are most noticeable at lower frequencies, and unfortunately smaller rooms are usually affected worse than larger rooms because the low-frequency modes are often quite intense, with little happening between them. In this case, one approach is to use tuned absorbers to damp down the energy peaks at the main modal frequencies, although some problems can also be avoided when planning the construction of the studio, by calculating ratios of room dimensions that produce the most evenly-spaced modes. Furthermore, near-field monitors with a restricted bass response may also be used, which will avoid exciting low-frequency modes.

To learn a little more about the best shape for a room, consider the worst possible shape: a cube. Inside a cube, all three axial modes occur at exactly the same frequencies, reinforcing each other to create noticeable peaks in the room's frequency response. Non-cuboid shapes are obviously more suitable, but if one dimension turns out to be exactly twice that of one of the others then modes will still occur at the same frequencies. Even dimensions which are apparently unrelated can cause modal pile-ups at some frequencies, purely by chance. In the past, a great deal of research has been undertaken to determine sets of ratios that minimise these undesirable peaks, and it's also possible to buy acoustic analysis software that will plot out the modes for any given dimension of room. Needless to say, this is certainly much easier than calculating each one manually.

Large gaps between modes create other problems, because the room response will dip noticeably in these places. In practice, you might find that musical pitches coinciding with these inter-mode gaps sound quieter in comparison with notes occurring in the rest of the spectrum. This is clearly something to avoid, because it will upset your perception of what you're hearing over the monitors and therefore lead to a less accurate mix.

In most rooms, once a threshold of around 300Hz or so has been reached the modes become so closely spaced that peaks or gaps cease to be a problem. Below this frequency, however, it's best not to have gaps between modes of more than around 20Hz. At the same time, closely-packed or coincident modes should also be avoided. The modal resonances in a typical studio tend to be around 5Hz wide, and the modal bandwidth is narrower in more reverberant rooms. Unfortunately, if a room is below a certain size it's impossible to arrive at dimensions where the low-frequency modal behaviour is ideal, so in the smaller home studio it's just one of those things that must be endured.

If you're so inclined, you can calculate the modal behaviour of a room by drawing a graph, plotting just the three axial modes against frequency and ignoring the tangential and oblique modes. (Calculating these modes is much more complicated, so if you're determined to do this I'd suggest that you get hold of some of the acoustic design software that's now available and let that do all the hard work. All you need to do is enter the room dimensions and it prints out the bad news!)

On a more practical level, modal problems in a room invariably have an adverse effect on the quality of reproduced speech, so much can be deduced about a room's mid-range performance simply by holding a conversation in it. If a room sounds good for speech it will probably also sound good for music, although there may still be low-frequency problems evident which occur below the natural frequency range of the human voice.

wall angles

It's a common misconception that building walls which aren't parallel will make the production of low-frequency standing waves less likely. In fact, low-frequency modes will still develop much as they did in a room with parallel walls, as their production depends on the mean distance between walls. Splaying the walls slightly will help reduce high-frequency flutter echoes caused by mid- and high-frequency sounds bouncing between two facing walls or floor and ceiling, but this problem is also controlled quite easily by using relatively small areas of acoustically absorbent material – such as acoustic foam – on either side of the listening position.

One architectural feature to avoid wherever possible is any form of concave structure, such as a bay window or a curved wall. These tend to focus reflected sound into one place, like a parabolic reflector, and this can seriously affect a room's acoustic performance when you're anywhere near the focal point. Convex or irregular surfaces are generally desirable, on the other hand, as they help to diffuse high frequencies, leading to a more even sound field.

room ratios

In practice, most home studio owners will have little control over the sizes of their rooms, but an unfavourable set of ratios need not be disastrous as long as monitors are chosen and positioned with care. Again, though, it's bad news if a room has dimensions that are exact multiples of each other, as all modes will tend to pile up at the same frequency.

design trends

Early studios were often constructed like padded cells, with walls lines with mineral wool, but this treatment produces a very dead mid-high acoustic, often with inadequate absorption at very low frequencies. The result is a room that booms at low frequencies but sounds unnaturally dead to speech.

Then came the introduction of the 'live-end/dead-end' studio, which deadened the sounds occurring at the monitor end of the studio by using a combination of absorption and geometry, while the back of the room was allowed to contribute some reflections. We've also seen the introduction of mathematically-designed scattering surfaces, and today's control rooms tend to incorporate a number of techniques with the aim of producing a better-balanced result. Most home studios will work fine with a few carefully-placed absorptive surfaces, although some additional bass trapping may be needed if the room is a little bass heavy. It's worth experimenting to discover other ways of using surfaces to diffuse or scatter sound in order to further randomise the reflections arriving at the listener.

Reverberation occurs in all untreated rooms, to the extent that music or speech sounds unnatural without it. In a studio control room, however, the reverberation characteristics need to be controlled within fairly close parameters if the end product is to be evaluated with any accuracy.

Reverberation is created whenever sound energy excites the room modes, and when the source of energy is removed the reverberation will decay at a rate determined by the geometry and absorbency of the room and its contents. Excessive low-frequency reverberation related to one dominating mode can cause serious problems for the engineer, who may end up using EQ in an attempt to fix a problem that doesn't really exist.

Reverberation time is conventionally defined as the time it takes for a sound to die away to a thousandth of its original sound level, and the resulting figure is referred to as 'T60', because the reverb time is then measured to the point at which the sound has decayed by 60dB. Ideal values of reverb time will depend on the size of the room and the type of material being auditioned (although the ideal time for a control room is likely to be around 0.3 seconds). There are formulas which use measurements of room dimensions and materials to calculate reverb times, but in smaller rooms the sound reflections don't even reach a sufficient level to create an even reverberant field, and so any calculations can only be approximate.

In a poorly-designed control room, problems arise because there are often different T60 values at different frequencies. If a room isn't designed with low-frequency reproduction in mind, it's invariably safer to use near-field monitors with limited low-end responses in order to avoid exciting the low-frequency room modes. The reverb time should be as constant as possible up to 8kHz or beyond, but a 'minimum intervention' approach is usually safest, because of the danger of trusting calculations based on small rooms and uncertain materials.

acoustic symmetry

The accurate reproduction of stereophonic sounds relies on both the room and the monitoring system being symmetrical, so it's good practice to try to balance the properties of facing (side) walls rather than put all absorbing material on one wall.

However, it's not always possible to treat opposing surfaces – such as floors and ceilings – in exactly the same way. If the floor is carpeted, it will absorb the higher frequencies very efficiently but will hardly affect the bass or lower-mid range at all. You could, however, mount bass traps in the ceiling which are designed to absorb the bass but reflect back the mid and higher frequencies absorbed by the carpet, although in practice it's often enough just to place a foam absorber on the ceiling above the mixing console, which will soak up any ceiling-to-listener mid- and high-frequency reflections from the monitors.

The only important thing that should be recognised is that the room should work for creating mixes that sound just as good when played on other systems outside the studio. Indeed, it's sometimes argued that, because most people listen to music in their living rooms, we should model our control rooms on a similar environment. However, the reality is that, in order to produce really good recordings, it's necessary to do so in a monitoring environment that's a little better than that enjoyed by the end user. Whichever approach you take, the area of the room around the monitor system must be as acoustically symmetrical as possible, and any large windows in a side wall must be balanced with an area with similar acoustic properties (varnished wood panels, for example) on the opposite wall. Practical suggestions on the acoustic treatment of studios are presented in chapter six.

In most small studios, early reflections from the speakers are kept away from the listening position with a combination of diffusion and geometry, and a combination of trapping and diffusion on the rear wall stops strong reflections from bouncing directly back to the sweet spot. However, this isn't the only approach, and the most effective solutions depend to some extent on the shape and size of the room.

flutter echo

Flutter echo is a distinctive ringing sound which is caused by echoes bouncing back and forth between hard parallel surfaces following a percussive sound, such as a handclap. To minimise flutter echoes occurring at the engineering position, it's usually enough to fix two or three foam acoustic tiles to each of the side walls at head height and level with the listening position.

acoustic absorbers

In the studio, it's most important to have well-behaved acoustics when working with speech, vocals or acoustic instruments, and if the room is less than ideal it's possible to set up local acoustic spaces by arranging acoustic screens or improvised absorbers. Absorbing mid and high frequencies is fairly straightforward (there are several acoustic tiles, foams and heavy drapes available that can effectively soak up frequencies above 300Hz), but the bass-end frequencies are more stubborn. Low-frequency sounds have long wavelengths, and a purely absorptive bass trap needs to be at least an eighth of a wavelength deep in order to be at all effective. At 50Hz this is something approaching three feet, and there aren't many home studios that can afford the space to cover a wall or two with a three-feet-thick (150-175kg/m^2 density) layer of mineral wool, such as rockwool. This type of bass trap has the advantage of working equally well at all frequencies, right down to its lower threshold, but in most small studios this isn't a realistic solution.

The other approach – which is understandably more popular – is to build a damped resonant structure that will absorb a significant proportion of a specific frequency band by converting it to heat via frictional losses. There are specialist materials available that are heavy, flexible and highly damped, and which lend themselves well to being used in a wide-band bass trap, such as mineral-loaded vinyl barrier matting or even lead-loaded materials.

Accurate results can be obtained with the use of a mineral-wool-filled trap between eight and twelve inches deep, with a membrane of barrier matting, and a broad-band bass trap of this type is shown in Figure 5.1. With such a high degree of damping, the action of the trap is almost like a floppy wall – the sound energy is expended in trying to vibrate the limp membrane, which is so well damped that the energy is largely absorbed. By covering the front with a layer of acoustic foam, the trap can be made effective over most of the audio spectrum.

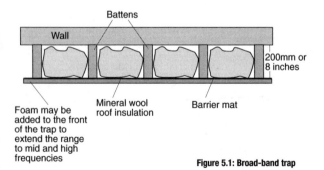

Figure 5.1: Broad-band trap

mid and high absorbers

One of the simplest absorbers to use at higher frequencies is simple open-cell foam, such as that used in furniture upholstery, and in fact expensive acoustic foam tiles are often only sculpted versions of this material. (For safety reasons, of course, only the fire-retardant type should be used.) The lowest frequency that will be effectively absorbed is dictated by the thickness of the foam, and in practice a one-inch thickness is most effective above 1kHz, while a four-inch layer is useful down to around 250Hz. The low-frequency absorption can also be improved by using a wooden frame to space the foam away from the wall by a few inches.

A similar absorber can be made by fixing a two-inch-thick slab of mineral wool to a frame two inches away from the wall. This should then be covered with open-weave fabric in order to stop the fibres from escaping into the air. (You should always wear a mask and gloves when handling mineral wool, and it should be installed in such a way that fibres can't escape into the air.) A mineral wool trap made like this should be effective down to around 250Hz or so.

The acoustic blankets used in broadcast work are similar to this, whereby layers of mineral wool reinforced with lightweight wire mesh are covered with fabric and hung from walls. The greater the airspace behind the blanket, the lower its threshold frequency of effectiveness.

Carpet isn't really thick enough to be effective at absorbing anything less than the high frequencies, and its absorbency drops off noticeably below 2kHz. There is a slight advantage to using a foam-backed carpet, however, and again its effectiveness can be extended by another octave or so if there is an airspace behind it. Even so, this is less effective than a wall treatment, unless another absorbent material is positioned behind the carpet.

Absorbing mid and high frequencies can be achieved by hanging heavy drapes a few inches from the wall. These should be generous enough to allow the material to hang in folds rather than being stretched tightly, and if these are hung on a rail in front of a reflective surface it's simple enough to draw back the drapes to convert a dead acoustic into a live one.

moveable screens

Portable acoustic screens are also useful because they can be used to modify the sound of a small part of a room for the recording of a vocal track, for example, or to record drums or acoustic guitar. These screens are generally built with a polished wood or synthetic laminate face on one side and about a four-inch-thick layer of mineral wool

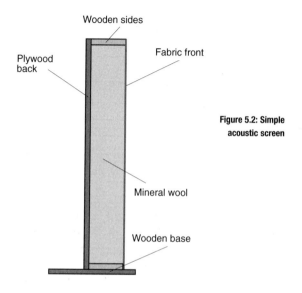

Wooden sides

Plywood back

Fabric front

Mineral wool

Wooden base

Figure 5.2: Simple acoustic screen

or foam absorber on the other. They are supported by simple wooden legs, and both live and dead environments can be created by simply facing either the hard or the absorbent side to the performer respectively. These screens are only effective down to around 250Hz on their absorbent side, but that's usually enough.

Drum booths may be set up by arranging a set of screens next to each other, with another screen balanced on the top to form a roof. Some screens have thick perspex windows in them to allow the drummer to see out. The live side is normally used to record drums, acoustic guitars and so on, and the dead side used for vocals. Figure 5.2 shows the construction of a simple acoustic screen.

summary

Absorbent traps can be useful in producing a more even acoustic environment, but only if applied so that a nominally consistent reverberation time is produced across the audio spectrum. People often use too much trapping when building their own studios, usually at mid and high frequencies, and this further emphasises low-frequency resonances, which are more difficult to cure. In any event, it's probably unwise to do anything irreversible before the carpets and equipment are installed in the studio, as these invariably make the room sound totally different to the way it did when it was empty.

Numerous advances in trap design have been made by specialists in the field, with the result that it's now possible to treat a completed room by adding just a few well-chosen panels in the right places. It's also possible to build panels with variable absorbency so that they can be adjusted *in situ*. Understandably, the designers of these traps are reluctant to reveal too much about their design!

practical acoustics

By listening to speech and music in a room it's possible to obtain a good impression of the room's acoustics. Even if the design isn't quite as good as you might have hoped, the human ear is capable of compensating for a multitude of inaccuracies, as long as it has some frame of reference, such as well-mixed commercial music played over the same monitors.

Although you wouldn't design a professional studio based only on instinct and subjective listening, you'd be surprised at how much you can improve the performance of a typical home studio by following a few simple guidelines. This is largely because the smaller monitors used in home studios don't have the same extended bass output as those used in commercial installations, and so less low-frequency energy is produced to excite the room modes down at those frequencies where the T60 may be longer than desirable. Also, the acoustics don't affect the perceived sound as much because smaller monitors can be positioned closer to the engineer, and so the ratio of direct to reverberant sound is higher.

the holistic approach

All of the wanted sound in a control room is reproduced by the loudspeaker system, and so when determining the acoustics of a control room it makes sense to start by considering what happens to the sound after it leaves the speakers. Monitor loudspeakers have a reasonably controlled directivity at mid and high frequencies, which generally means that most of the sound emerges as a cone of energy from the front of the box. Unfortunately, at lower frequencies this cone widens considerably, and at very low frequencies the speaker cabinet effectively becomes an omnidirectional radiator, emitting almost as much energy from the back and the sides as from the front. However, it's generally both impractical and undesirable to try and absorb all of the sound that misses the listener and instead hits a surface in the room. Some studios are built to be virtually anechoic (literally echoless) chambers, but most people find these kind of rooms oppressive, and because so much energy is being absorbed by the surroundings a very powerful monitor system is required to obtain the necessary sound level. Anechoic or completely absorbent control rooms are unpleasant places in which to work because speech within them sounds very dry and quiet, as there are no wall reflections to breathe life into it.

controlling reflections

In a normal listening environment, sound produced by the speakers is reflected from walls and other surfaces in ways that can be both musically constructive and destructive, and so when designing a good control room the trick is to try to avoid building an environment that produces the wrong type of reflections while at the same time encouraging and controlling the desired variety. A well-diffused reverberation with an reverb time of around 0.3 seconds is generally considered to be about right for professional control rooms, although in a home studio you might be able to get away with a slightly longer value.

Well-diffused and spectrally-neutral reflections arriving very shortly after the original sound often end up combining with it, increasing its subjective level. However, for the best results these reflections should be at least 10dB lower in level than the direct sound, and this usually means avoiding reflections which originate from surfaces near the speakers themselves, as well as those which are produced by materials that only reflect a part of the audio spectrum. Longer delays caused by reflections in larger rooms (ie longer than around 40ms) are undesirable, being plainly audible as slap-back echoes. This would correspond to a front-to-back room distance of around 20 feet (6 metres).

highs and lows

It helps to understand what's going on if we split the audio spectrum into two bands. Frequencies in a typical room up to around 300Hz are influenced mainly by modes and by the physical position of the monitors within the room, while most of the problems experienced at higher frequencies are associated with multiple reflection paths.

Looking at the loudspeaker position first, from Figure 6.1 it's clear that, if a speaker is positioned on a stand away from the walls, sound from the back and sides of the cabinet will reach the side and rear walls and then reflect back into the room. This is known as the speaker boundary effect, and the best way to imagine this is to visualise the walls as being covered with mirrors. Everywhere that you can see a reflection of the monitor, a phantom sound source will be created. Because the walls aren't perfectly reflective to sound, and because the sound radiating from the sides and the back of the speaker is mainly of quite a low frequency, the phantom sources are effectively filtered out so that only low frequencies come back to the speaker. These low-pass-filtered reflections then combine with the direct low-frequency energy emitted from the front of the speaker, as shown in Figure 6.2.

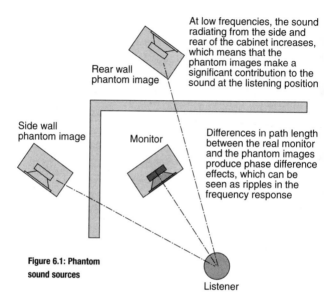

At low frequencies, the sound radiating from the side and rear of the cabinet increases, which means that the phantom images make a significant contribution to the sound at the listening position

Rear wall phantom image

Side wall phantom image

Monitor

Differences in path length between the real monitor and the phantom images produce phase difference effects, which can be seen as ripples in the frequency response

Figure 6.1: Phantom sound sources

Listener

The reflected sound will never be exactly in phase with the direct sound because of the distance which it has to travel, but where the wavelengths are long (ie at very low frequencies) they're sufficiently in phase to cause some constructive interference. In simple terms, this means that positioning a speaker close to a solid wall will cause an increase in bass energy, as some of the low-frequency energy normally lost from the back of the cabinet is reflected back to the listener. As the frequency increases, the difference in the path length between the direct and reflected sound will correspond to a different number of wavelengths, so that, at some frequencies, the direct and reflected sounds will combine while at others they will cancel each other out. This is why the amplitude response in the graph in Figure 6.2 shows a series of ripples.

If the speaker is placed near a corner, reflections from both the rear and side walls combine with each other to produce a greater bass rise and more pronounced ripples in the low-frequency response, and if the floor reflections are also included then this bass rise can be very significant. While some people might view this as a simple way to obtain 'free' extra bass, the deep

Figure 6.2: Speaker boundary effec

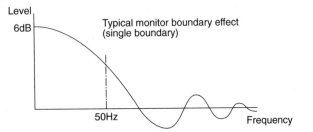

ripples in the low-frequency response can lead to problematic hot and dead spots in the bass end. The only way to avoid this is to keep monitor speakers away from corners and to try to randomise the distances between the speaker cabinet and the nearby walls. For this reason, in small studios it's often best to place the monitors along the longest wall and as far away from the corners as possible rather than along the shortest wall, where they will be nearer the corners. If the speakers are placed at exactly the same distance from the rear wall, the side wall and the floor, the bass boost produced at very low frequencies can be up to 18dB, with huge ripples extending into the bottom couple of octaves of the monitor's response.

The only practical way of utilising the energy radiated from the rear of the speaker cabinet without incurring problems with phase difference is to actually mount the speaker monitor flush with the wall, which is why the monitoring systems in many large studios are built into the front wall. In this way, all of the low-frequency energy is forced to radiate into a 180° space, rather than being allowed to radiate into a 360° space; and because there is no distance between the monitor and the boundary, there is an almost perfect doubling of low-frequency efficiency, with no ripples.

To obtain a flat frequency response from flush-mounted speakers, the monitors themselves must be designed with a corresponding drop in low-frequency efficiency so that the net result is flat. On the other hand, purpose-built stand-mounted speakers are designed on the assumption that they will be positioned some distance away from the boundary, which is why many manufacturers include instructions on how to position their monitors relative to walls. It's also for this reason that some active monitors are built with bass-end tailoring controls in order to help compensate for the effects of positioning.

geometry

Placing speakers in their optimum position in relation to the boundaries of a room will minimise anomalies produced by a low-frequency response, but it's also necessary to minimise the level of any early reflections that may be produced by the sound emitted from the front of the speaker striking a nearby surface and reflecting back to the listener. In a professional studio equipped with flush-mounted monitors, this is often achieved by combining areas of absorption with wall and ceiling geometries that have been carefully designed so that any reflections that can't be avoided are deflected away from the listening position.

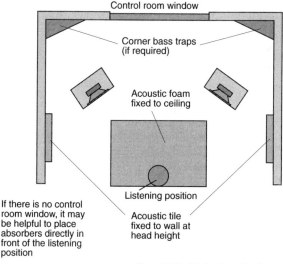

Figure 6.3: Positioning foam absorbers

This is rarely practical in the home studio, especially if stand-mounted monitors are used, but it's possible to stick relatively simple mid- and high-frequency-absorbent materials on the walls and ceiling to intercept the strongest reflections, and this is a very simple and cheap procedure. Figure 6.3 illustrates how this can be done. If you're not sure exactly where to stick them, get a friend to hold a mirror against the studio wall. If you can see the reflection of the monitor in the mirror from your normal listening position, you should place your acoustic tile so that the image would be in the centre of the tile. An area of one square metre of tile on each side wall is generally quite adequate, but if you use the thickest type you can get it will be effective to a lower frequency than the thinner type – something around 100mm thick is ideal. The ceiling should be tiled in the same way.

This approach to minimising powerful early reflections is part of the so-called live-end/dead-end control room design philosophy, which (with the exception of a few changes) is still the most common in modern control room design. In this design, the speakers are located at the dead end of the room (designed to produce minimal early reflections), and the other (live) end of the room is designed to scatter reflected energy back into the room as randomly and diffuse as possible. What you don't want is a solid, flat back wall that reflects the sound of the monitors back as a coherent echo. Commercial studios are designed with angled sections of rear wall, semi-cylindrical constructions and purpose-made diffusers. In the home studio it's possible to break up reflections by lining the rear wall with storage shelves, and a soft sofa across the back of the room will also provide some welcome low-frequency absorption.

small studios

This live-end/dead-end approach has to be modified further for small studios, because in rooms where there isn't a great distance between the front and rear walls it generally isn't possible to break up the reflections from the rear wall to a sufficient degree, and because of the small distances involved the reflections may be stronger than desirable. In such cases, it's common practice to employ a mixture of heavy trapping and diffusion on the rear wall. For example, a mineral wool trap covered with barrier matting, like that described in chapter five, is both effective and relatively easy to build.

other trapping

When it comes to positioning other trapping that may be required, the most important thing to remember is to keep the room as acoustically symmetrical as possible. Bass traps are usually fitted in corners, as these are the points at which the main room modes are anchored, and a simple setup may only required the addition of two rear-corner floppy membrane traps, with the area between them taken up by scattering surfaces, such as shelving. On the other hand, if you've decided to trap the entire back wall you probably won't need any additional bass trapping.

If larger monitors are being used and the boundary reflections are causing problems, it may also be desirable to fit bass traps in the front corners of the studio or directly behind the monitors. However, in a typical home studio equipped with suitable near-field monitors, it's often possible to get away with using little or no bass trapping, other than that provided by soft furnishings.

monitoring

No matter how sophisticated your recording equipment or your instruments, the final judgement of a track has to be made by ear, and without a good monitoring system this judgement cannot be made with any degree of accuracy. The sole aim of a studio monitoring system is to provide an accurate point of reference, so that the mixing engineer can be confident that his or her work is going to sound as intended. This apparently modest requirement isn't as straightforward as it seems, however, because there's no such thing as a standard monitor loudspeaker, and even if there were such a thing it would always sound different depending on the environment in which it was used, its position within that environment and even on the type of amplifier which was used to drive it. To make matters worse, the studio engineer doesn't know what speaker system will be employed by the end user, because these too are all different – some users will have top-of-the-range hi-fi systems, while others will be listening on cheap music centres or car radios.

what is a monitor?

What exactly do we mean when we refer to an accurate monitor loudspeaker? And what's the difference between a monitor loudspeaker and a hi-fi loudspeaker? An accurate speaker might be defined as one that faithfully reproduces the entire audio spectrum (allowing for some compromise at the bass end, due to size restrictions) with the minimum of distortion or coloration. Even this isn't as simple as it seems, however, because, while some speakers might come close to this ideal when the listener is standing right in front of them, their off-axis performance might be far from accurate. If you're going to set up the speakers so that they're pointing directly at you (as, indeed, you always should), why then should you worry about off-axis accuracy?

reflections

It's a fact of life that sound bounces, and what we hear when we listen to music through a pair of loudspeakers is a combination of the direct (on-axis) sound combined with a proportion of the indirect (off-axis) sound after it has reflected from the walls and other objects within the room. It doesn't matter how accurate the on-axis sound is; if the the off-axis sound is grossly inaccurate then it stands to reason that any reflected sound we hear will also be horribly inaccurate. It's largely because of the differences in off-axis performance that two similarly-specified loudspeakers can sound so different in the same room. In an ideal world, the only discernible difference that listeners should notice as they move off-axis from a loudspeaker is a drop in sound levels, but in reality the high frequencies will drop away first, and if the speaker is a particularly bad one it can change drastically.

Having reached the conclusion that a good loudspeaker must be accurate both on and off axis, what's the difference between a studio monitor and a good hi-fi speaker? To start with, many so-called hi-fi speakers are nothing of the kind, and indeed many are designed with deliberate inaccuracies to make them sound more impressive. For example, a small cabinet usually signifies a limited bass response; however, by tuning the cabinet so that it accentuates the area of the spectrum located at around 80Hz, bass drums and bass guitars can be given the illusion of having more punch and depth. This is fine in a bedsit or in the car, but if you perform a mix on speaker like this you'll end up trying to compensate for the character of the speakers. Your mix will then sound wrong when played on any other speaker system.

power handling

The main attribute of a studio monitor is that, as long as it's sufficiently accurate both on and off axis, it can handle a considerable amount of power and produce very high SPLs (Sound Pressure Levels). Although it isn't necessary to monitor at high volumes, many studio engineers like to be able to hear a solo bass drum and hear it at the same level as that at which the drummer is playing it, which can peak at somewhere around 300 watts or more! Similarly, if you're recording a full symphony orchestra and want to hear it played back at its natural volume, you're going to need hugely powerful monitors. It may not be necessary to monitor at anywhere near that volume at home, but even home monitors need to be quite robust in order to withstand the onslaught of uncompressed drum machines and high-pitched, high-energy synth sounds.

the room

Many professional monitoring systems are designed to work in a particular room, and if a studio is being built from scratch the room and monitors may be designed together as a complete system. And they *are* a system, because the room has a very profound effect on the overall sound. Monitors are generally built into the walls in larger studios, and this setup is known as soffit mounting. (Speakers designed for conventional stand mounting should not be soffit mounted, as the resulting bass performance will be incorrect.)

Another very important point to keep in mind is that you can't expect to generate very deep bass in a small room. Indeed, unless the room is very large, using full-range loudspeakers will only produce a confused and inaccurate bass response, even though the speakers themselves may be quite accurate, because the dimensions of the room will be too small to accommodate the wavelengths of the lower notes.

A practical option is to use a pair of speakers that has a flat response down to around 60-70Hz and then rolls off gradually towards the low end of the spectrum. In this case the room won't affect the bass end quite as much. A good two-way system with a bass driver of between six and ten inches in diameter is usually more than adequate for use in a home studio, and the models with soft-dome tweeters produce a smoother and more natural sound than those which use metal or plastic tweeters. Horn loudspeakers enjoy no advantages at all when monitoring at low to medium levels; their main advantage is that they can produce high sound levels, but the trade-off is higher distortion, particularly in the upper mid and treble regions.

position

It's not just the size of a room that's important but also the positioning of the speakers. At mid and high frequencies the sound radiates from a loudspeaker in a cone shape, but at low frequencies the radiation pattern becomes omnidirectional, with almost as much energy being directed backwards as forwards. This low-frequency energy will then proceed to bounce off the walls adjacent to and immediately behind the speakers, resulting in an increase in the perceived bass level within the room, which itself is another good reason to choose speakers with a gentle bass roll-off.

The distances between the speaker and the nearer surfaces should ideally be as random as possible, in order to stop all of the reflections combining at the same frequency. The worst thing that you can do is put a speaker in a corner, halfway between the floor and the ceiling, because this will produce a bass response interspersed with large peaks and troughs. This setup will result in some bass notes sounding much too loud and others being unusually quiet, as described in more detail in chapter six. If it's possible to make the distances between the speaker and the nearest two walls, the floor and the ceiling all different, the reflections will combine in a more random fashion, producing a smoother bass response with less severe peaks and dips. As a rule, try to keep speakers at least a foot from the wall in front of you, and at least 18 inches from the side walls. In rectangular rooms, it's usually preferable to keep the speakers as far away from the corners and side walls as possible by setting them up along the longest wall, because this will reduce both the intensity of any reflections reaching the listener and the extent to which the direct sound is compromised by the reflected sound.

It's currently fashionable to mount monitors on the meter bridge of a mixing console, but this practise isn't without its problems; because the speakers are so close to the console, a lot of what's heard is sound reflected from the surface of the console, and when this is combined with the direct sound from the speakers it creates peaks and dips in the mid range. It's a much better idea to erect the speakers on stands a little way behind the desk.

Because speakers are designed to be at their most accurate when used on axis, it's important that the tweeters are pointed towards the head of the listener. It's also important to ensure that the speakers don't rattle or vibrate on their stands, and although it's not

**Figure 7.1: Speaker angle relative to
listening position**

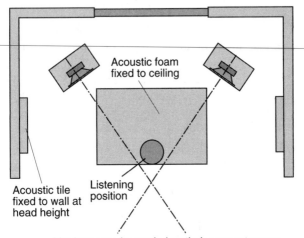

Acoustic foam
fixed to ceiling

Acoustic tile
fixed to wall at
head height

Listening
position

Monitors may be angled so their axes converge
just behind the listening position. This produces a
reasonably accurate stereo image for other
musicians standing just behind the mix engineer
as well as for the engineer

really necessary to use spiked speaker stands it
sometimes helps to rest the speaker cabinets on top of
four blobs of Blu Tac. Figure 7.1 demonstrates the
optimum speaker setup for a home studio. Note that
the tweeter axes converge slightly behind the
listener's head in order to allow a wide listening angle
for those standing directly behind the engineer.

amplifier power

Conventional wisdom used to suggest that buying a small power amplifier was the best way of protecting speakers from being overloaded, but in recent years the reverse has been proven to be true. Most speakers will withstand short periods of being overloaded, as long as the input signal isn't unduly distorted or clipped. However, an under-powered amplifier can easily be driven into clipping, which results in a harmonically rich and clipped waveform being fed into the tweeters. As well as sounding disgusting, this can easily overheat the tweeter's voice coil and cause it to burn out.

The best option is to use the largest amplifier recommended for your speakers, rather than the smallest, and ideally one that has clip indicators to indicate when you're running out of headroom.

speaker wiring

While it's undeniably true that using flimsy cable will compromise the sound of your speakers, there is really very little difference between one heavy-duty cable and another compared to all of the other variables in your studio. You should always use the heaviest speaker cable practical, ideally rated at ten amps or more, but it's not worth wasting money on fancy hi-fi cable. However, it's a good idea to keep speaker cables as short as possible, and to ensure that both speaker leads are the same length. You should also make sure that the speakers are wired in phase (ie red terminal on the amplifier to red terminal on the speaker), and check that the ends of the cables are firmly clamped at both ends.

studio wiring

This chapter investigates the theory behind wiring up your own studio, and offers some practical suggestions for the arrangement of patchbays and mixing desks. This subject is covered in greater detail in the book *basic MIXERS*, also in this series.

If your system is based around a hardware multitrack mixer with analogue I/O (input/output), there will probably be some routing tasks that can't be performed by using only the controls on the mixer, and it's here that patchbays become useful. Patchbays are available in two basic configurations: normalised and non-normalised. Normalised patchbays are equipped with switch contacts so that the signal flow is unbroken when the patchbay sockets are empty, whereas non-normalised patchbays can be considered as the audio equivalent of extension cables, allowing you to bring out existing connections to a more convenient location. Professional studios generally use miniature bantam jack patchbays, but in the home studio – where lots of musical instruments and processors must be interfaced, most of which use standard quarter-inch jacks – a quarter-inch jack patchbay makes more sense.

Jack patchbays may be unbalanced or balanced, with either mono or stereo jacks respectively, and in most instances connection to the rear of the patchbay is again achieved with jacks. Patchbays can help you operate more smoothly, even in a small studio, by bringing out to a central point things like insert points, effects sends and returns and the inputs for effects and processors. However, as long as the jack sockets on your mixer are reasonably accessible, there's no reason to use a patchbay if a connection is are rarely – if ever – changed.

Note, however, that the convention for patchbay wiring requires that the bottom socket of a pair should be the input and the top socket the output. Because some commercial patchbays are provided in a semi-normalised state (ie the signal path is only broken when something is plugged into the bottom socket), if you use them the other way up they won't work on those occasions when you only want to take a feed from the insert send without breaking the signal path.

Normalised patchbays are used in those situations where a signal path has to be interrupted in order to either insert another audio processor into the signal chain or to divert an input or output somewhere else. Insert points must always be normalised, but normalised patchbays are also useful for connecting such things as multitrack recorder inputs and outputs to the mixer, as they provide you with the flexibility to patch in a different multitrack machine or route mic pre-amps directly to tape without going through the mixer.

The inputs and outputs of effects processors should be connected to a non-normalised patchbay, unless you want to set up a default system so that certain effects units are routed back to certain mixer channels or effects returns. It's a good idea to plan patchbays so that, when no patch cables are inserted, you have a default setup which allows you to perform a variety of basic tasks without having to plug in any patch cables at all. This kind of setup only requires patching when you have to insert a processor or do something a little out of the ordinary.

to patch or not to patch

Technically speaking, the signal path is cleaner without a patchbay because there are fewer resistive contacts through which the signal has to travel (every plug and socket represents a resistive contact), so if you can organise your system to keep patching to a minimum not only will you save money but you'll also reduce the risk of

the signal degrading. The trick of building a smooth-running patchbay, of course, is planning. It's worth spending an evening or two with a notepad and pencil, and in a bigger studio it's even more important that the patching system is designed properly.

If you have a large setup, it's worth considering using foil-screened cable or some other suitable small-diameter screened cable to wire up your patchbay, or you might find that your wiring harness becomes incredibly bulky. For smaller systems, it should be enough to use regular screened instrument or mic cables, or even ready-made moulded jacks.

what to patch?

You can't really pre-wire processors such as compressors or gates because you don't know in which mixer channel you'll need to use them (unless you're the only person who uses the studio, and you always work in exactly the same way). Consequently, most studio patching systems bring out all of a mixer's channel, group and master stereo insert points to semi-normalised patchbays. The majority of mixers used in home studios use unbalanced insert points, through which a stereo jack carries both the send and return signal, so you'll need a normalised mono patchbay and a whole bunch of Y-leads (cables with stereo jacks at one end and two mono jacks at the other). There is a guide to wiring connectors in the appendix of this book, and you may also find this kind of information in your mixer handbook. It's possible to buy your own Y-leads, but it's far cheaper to make your own, if you can face the prospect of soldering.

As well as insert points, it's also useful to bring out both aux sends and returns to the patchbay, along with effects and processor inputs and outputs (not forgetting any side-chain access points). If you have a console with plenty of aux sends and you only own two effects units it may make sense to wire in these permanently, but on a non-normalised patchbay it's still worth bringing out the remaining sends for those occasions when a friend brings over another processor.

Most studios use at least two types of stereo machine, often in the form of a DAT recorder and a cassette deck or MiniDisc recorder, and if you perform any kind of commercial work you may also have an open-reel analogue mastering machine. If your mixer doesn't cater for more than one mastering machine, the connections for the other machines and the mixer stereo output will have to come out to patch points so that they can be connected as required.

In my own system I've used a normalised patching system so that, when nothing is plugged into the patchbay, the mixer output feeds into three tape machines at once. However, when a plug is connected to the input of one of the machines, it's isolated from the mixer output. In this way I can mix directly onto any of the three machines (or all three at once, for that matter), but it's also easy to patch the output of one machine back to the input of another if you need to do any copying. Similarly, the output of any tape machine can be patched into a mixer input so that taped sounds can then be added to a mix.

mixer inputs

While it's quite possible to plug equipment directly into the line input sockets on a mixer, if you're using a non-normalised patchbay it's probably more convenient to bring out the input channels. If you have direct channel outputs, and you want to use them, it's possible to use a single patchbay with the line inputs on the bottom row and the direct outputs on the top row. If you don't have direct outputs, or you don't need to use them, it's possible to use both rows of the patchbay as inputs rather than adhering rigidly to convention.

At this stage, it's also worth looking at audio outs running from MIDI instruments. If these are normally connected to specific mixer channels it may be a good idea to use a normalised patchbay, as this would make it possible to break into the signal chain and take a synth output or use a mixer input without having to unplug anything. Having said that, however, if you're confident that you won't need to change your patching configuration then there's a lot to be said for not having a patchbay at all.

MIDI patching

With MIDI, if you have a lot of modules hooked up to your system, or if you're in the habit of working with more than one type of sequencer, then a simple, mechanical MIDI patchbay can prove to be very handy. These devices are simple panels which connect up to your system with DIN connectors, and there are usually duplicate DIN connectors on the back of them so they can be wired up using standard MIDI leads. Even if you don't need one of these to handle the MIDI feeds to your instruments, it makes things a lot easier if you use one for your MIDI synth outputs, as this will make it an easy task to patch a synth back into your computer's MIDI input for editing purposes. Programmable MIDI patchbays are available, of course, but in most home studios a manual system should be quite adequate.

mic wiring

In a studio devoted mainly to MIDI, it's hardly worth having any special provision for one or two mics – you may as well plug them directly into the mixer whenever you need them. However, in a larger studio, or in one equipped with a separate playing area, it pays to run a balanced multicore from the mixer mic inputs to a wall box fitted with balanced XLR sockets. The multicore should comprise individually-screened and balanced pairs, and should be run away from mains cables if at all possible. If eight or more mic lines are needed, multicore cable is the most convenient medium through which to achieve this.

labelling

It's important to label your patchbay clearly, but today's patchbays are so small that this isn't always easy to achieve. Using handwritten labels is as good a way of doing this as anything, if you have a fine pen and neat handwriting.

Even a relatively small studio can become a wiring nightmare if you don't keep track of your connections, so it's a good idea to label all leads and plugs as they are connected up – sticky paper labels protected by sellotape are usually adequate. It's also vitally important to have clear access to the back of a patchbay (as I discovered to my cost when I once built a system that could only be accessed by removing the patchbay from the front!)

It may also be helpful to use a racking system for your patchbay that's a little larger than necessary in order to have somewhere to coil up all the extra cable that somehow seems to accumulate. In a perfect world all cable harnesses would be exactly the right length, but it's usually a good idea to have a few feet more cable than necessary, as this will provide some much-needed flexibility if you decide to change your studio's layout.

Because most patchbay connections run to the mixer, it makes sense to keep the patchbay as close to the mixer as possible. Even so, the location of your effects rack will also be important because all effects ins and outs will also end up in the patchbay. In my own studio I've built a combined patchbay and effects rack that sits right alongside the mixer so that only the MIDI rack and the wiring harnesses of the multitrack DAT machine are visible. In theory, shorter cable runs will reduce the risk of interference and crosstalk, but equally important is that fact that using less cable will cost you less money!

mains wiring

When setting up a high-quality home studio, the first thing that should be consided is the location of the electricity supply. Although simply plugging everything into the nearest power point and hoping for the best might be acceptable for the bedroom recordist, this practise is prey to electrical interference from other systems in the house. Equally important is the fact that even a modest studio installation may include literally dozens of mains plugs, and trying to shoehorn all of these into one wall socket using domestic distribution boards or adaptors is simply asking for trouble. Even if the total load on the socket doesn't exceed the stipulated maximum (which in the UK is a maximum of 13 amps per socket), if you're using a mixture of cheap distribution boards and adaptors then you're risking intermittent mains connections, which can arc and cause interference. If you're wondering why this should be the case, look inside a typical plastic distribution board and you'll see that the sockets are actually small pieces of metal crimped onto rigid wire buss bars. Once these have been used a few times the sockets lose their spring and fail to make good contact with the plug. Because these faults are likely to be intermittent, any resulting interference may take a lot of tracking down.

the mains supply

Usually, the main cause of concern isn't the mains circuit overloading but rather interference and mains hum caused by inappropriate wiring. Most studio equipment takes relatively little current, and the needs of the average home studio can often be supplied by just one or two outlets. Most modern houses are wired to a ring main, where the main electrical cabling forms a complete loop, starting and finishing at the fuse box.

If you're planning to implement a new system of mains wiring, you should specify a separate consumer unit and ring main for your studio area, and larger facilities should have two mains supplies fitted – one for the 'clean' audio/computer supply and one for 'dirty' power, such as heating, lighting and coffee machines. A consumer unit is the modern equivalent of a fuse box, but it's more likely to be equipped with resettable trip switches.

Using a separate consumer unit which is fed from the building's main fuse box also provides a degree of natural interference rejection, helping to minimise the clicks and buzzes caused by appliances such as fridges, thermostats and central heating systems. If these continue to break through onto your audio, hire an electrician to fit suppressors to the offending items.

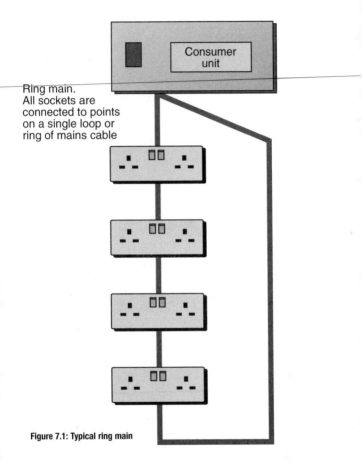

Ring main.
All sockets are
connected to points
on a single loop or
ring of mains cable

Figure 7.1: Typical ring main

Unless you know what you're doing, you should have the supply installed by a qualified electrician, and make sure that it complies with local building regulations. Even though studio equipment takes relatively little current, the lower the impedance of the wiring the better, and it may be worthwhile to ask the electrician to use the heaviest-duty cable he can. This can help keep down outside interference, and it will also help prevent any deterioration in sound quality which might otherwise occur when the mains supply to one piece of equipment is modulated by the mains current taken by current-hungry equipment, such as power amplifiers.

hum

All mains cables should be run together as far as is possible, and it helps if they can be run around the top of the room with drops to the various sockets. The logic behind this is that it keeps the mains as far as possible from your signal cables, which reduces the risk of picking up hum. It may help to run the cable in metal rather than plastic conduit, and you should ensure that the conduit is earthed – ask the electrician to check the earthing spike, which forms the contact between your mains earth and the planet below. If it isn't providing a low enough path of impedance, consider getting a longer one fitted. Figure 8.1 shows a typical ring main configuration.

distribution

Always plan for as many wall sockets as you can squeeze in, but be prepared for the fact that you still won't have enough! If you're not sure about the power consumed by your equipment, the figure should be either quoted in the handbook or marked on the back of the case. Add these figures together and make sure that you're not connecting more than the allowed amount to any individual socket, and that the total doesn't exceed the rating of the fuse or trip in the consumer unit.

In practice, lighting and heating demands much more power than audio equipment, and ideally should be run from a separate 'dirty' circuit. In order to split the power from a pair of mains outlets to drive more studio equipment, it's best to either buy a distribution board or make one up using commercial-grade, metal-cased switched mains sockets. By mounting the distribution boards in the backs of equipment racks, the amount of exposed cabling can be kept to a minimum.

Computers should ideally be fed to the audio from a different spur, and certainly shouldn't be fed from a 'dirty' supply because the system will be more likely to crash. It may be wise to invest in a computer mains filter; although they provide only limited protection, they will help to filter out mains spikes and surges.

chapter 9

a final word

This final chapter summarises the various stages you need to go through when designing a small studio, and – accepting that relatively few structural changes can be made in most home studios – I'm also including a few alternative ways of working that might help to work around some problems. The most important criteria is usually soundproofing, especially in residential areas, and while restrictions in space or budget may make it impossible to cure this problem completely, you'll almost certainly be able to make a significant improvement without having to rip the house apart or spend a fortune.

the source of noise

It's a generally accepted fact that the sound isolation achieved in a typical house is unlikely ever to be perfect, without undertaking major restructuring work. However, you may be able to meet the problem halfway by generating less noise in the first place. The choice of monitors is important here, as these speakers will produce most of the noise. Near-field monitors are a wise choice for the small studio, and for a number of reasons. Firstly, with these it's possible to monitor at quite a low level, which would be difficult with a system located further away from the listener, and so the effect of the room's acoustic is therefore minimised and the amount of sound being generated in the first place is much lower. Furthermore, near-field monitors generally produce less deep bass frequencies than large, full-range monitors, and while bass may be appealing, if it's produced in a small or untreated room it's likely to be very misleading. It's much better to configure the monitor's bass response to the room in order to obtain a more accurate impression of the fine tuning in a particular mix. As far as noise is concerned, low frequencies cause the most problems, and so by cutting down on the amount of bass your studio produces you will also cut down on the nuisance factor of your monitoring system.

If your system is still very noisy, and you find that you can't work late at night without disturbing your neighbours, you should still be able to carry out at least some of your recording by wearing headphones and leave mixing until daylight hours, when the noise produced by your monitors will be less problematic.

If your equipment is too noisy, this can invariably be improved if it's isolated from the floor of the room – particularly if the floor is made of wood. I once heard a story about one frustrated project studio owner who replaced his traditional drum kit with a set of electronic pads, only to find that the physical thump of the bass drum pedal still sounded loud and clear in the room below. You may want to try mounting instrument amplifiers on rubber foam, or even inflated inner tubes, which may help in cutting down structurally-borne sound. Drum kits are a different matter, however, and although the amount of sound leakage can be reduced by positioning the kit on a plinth built like a section of floating floor, anyone expecting to get away with constant drumming in a flat or apartment without upsetting the neighbours is doomed to a life of eternal disappointment!

Rock guitars may now be DI'd (Direct Injected) in a quite satisfactory manner by way of speaker simulators or dedicated recording pre-amps. These speaker simulators plug directly into the speaker outlet (or occasionally the pre-amp output) of an instrument amplifier and filter the sound in a way which imitates the way in which a speaker would impart its own coloration. The output is a low-level signal which can be DI'd directly into a mixing console, and one of the great advantages of this approach (apart from avoiding any problems with noise) is that the sound produced by the monitors is exactly the sound that's being recorded on the tape. While purists still prefer to mic up their amps, some modern recording pre-amps are extremely good, especially those that are constructed using digital physical modelling. If you must use an amp, however, try to use a small-valve practice combo, as often these not only record better (and sound bigger) than a large stack but also minimise noise and spill.

cheap and dirty acoustics

While the practise of soundproofing follows fairly predictable physical rules, acoustic treatment is less easily pinned down in mathematical terms. Although there are well-documented physical laws governing the way in which sound is absorbed and reflected, in a typical home studio there are so many variables that come into play that it's virtually impossible to calculate how a room will behave acoustically, and this is perhaps why so many people consider acoustic design to be as much an art as a science. Even if it were possible to be absolutely certain about the acoustic properties of all of the materials present in a room, the acoustics would still change significantly as soon as equipment and furniture was introduced.

There is also some disagreement concerning what actually constitutes the ideal monitoring environment, but ultimately it's important to bear in mind that the end result of our efforts is likely to be a CD or cassette, played over fairly small speakers in an acoustically imperfect domestic room or in a car. One thing that is certain, however, is that few people will be listening in acoustically perfect control rooms with monitors the size of cupboards. The most important thing is to have a symmetrical room, in which the reverb time is well controlled and nominal even across the audio spectrum. Strong early reflections from the monitors should also be avoided.

choosing a monitor

While it's important to listen to big-budget commercial mixes over full-range speakers to confirm what's going on right at the bottom of the audio spectrum, a pair of your average domestic hi-fi speakers may well miss out the lowest octave completely. Unless the control room is large enough, and designed to handle full-range monitors, the results are likely to be more misleading than simply relying on near-field speakers. Even when a mix can be checked on a full-range monitor system, it's still a good idea to double check that it sounds as you think it does on a domestic two-way speaker – hence the tendency to use compact, two-way devices as near-field monitors. Another advantage of using near-field monitoring is that the weaker bass end will leave the vulnerable mid range more exposed, and so any errors or distortions can be picked up more easily. This is very important, because the strong bass produced by full-range monitors can easily overpower and obscure the mid range.

Whatever the room, and whatever the monitor system being used, the way in which your ears evaluate music deteriorates with time and with monitoring level, so it's essential to have some sort of reference against which to compare your mixes. It's good practice to play some pre-recorded material over the system before mixing in order to have a control. It's well known amongst studio engineers that adding high-end EQ or processing the sound with an exciter decreases the ear's sensitivity to the actual amount of top end in a mix, so if you don't regularly compare your mix with some kind of control track you could end up with a track with some very strange EQ'ing. Not all CDs are recorded as well as they should be, but it should be possible to pick out a few reference tracks that both sound good and cover the same style of music as that on which you intend to work.

realistic aims

Commercial control rooms are designed to meet criteria that are simply not achievable in smaller or home studios. They are equipped with inner shells designed with non-parallel walls, specially-shaped ceilings and carefully-calculated trapping. If you're thinking of setting up a home studio or a small-scale commercial facility, you may have to adapt a rectangular room of less than optimum proportions. This isn't always as bad as it seems, however, because this describes exactly a typical living room, and this is where most recorded music is heard. In reality, with a little work most living rooms can sound acceptable, as long as an appropriate speaker system is installed.

There is a school of thought which suggests that most of the acoustic problems present in a studio are brought about by the physical needs of the studio space – in other words, a perfectly acceptable room is acoustically spoiled by emptying it of furniture and filling it with equipment. This makes some kind of sense, as soft furnishings both diffuse and absorb sound, while studio equipment is usually a collection of hard, flat, reflective surfaces.

With a little thought, many of these undesirable effects can be minimised. For example, carpeting the floor will help damp down ringing, and will also shorten the overall reverb time, while a soft sofa positioned at the back will help soak up reflections and damp resonances, and will also provide clients with somewhere to sit. An environment that's too live can by treated by hanging heavy drapes or rugs a few inches from the wall, but don't fall into the trap of damping the high end so much that the bottom booms out of control.

Bass trapping probably isn't vital, as long as a pair of speakers with a smooth bass roll-off are used and the room has some large soft furnishings. Wooden floors and plasterboard linings in a room also helps to trap out some of the bass. A monitor designed to roll off gradually below 80Hz or so will work much better in an untrapped room than one which uses heavily-tuned porting to prop up the bass down to around 50Hz or so but then cuts off rapidly.

There's one important aspect of studio performance that can't be designed in, however: your own hearing. Good engineers can make effective mixes on the most rudimentary equipment as long as they're aware of its limitations and they occasionally compare their work with known reference recordings. You should avoid the temptation to monitor at high levels for long periods of time, as this will not only cloud your judgment and affect your perception of the musical balance but it can also cause permanent hearing damage. As a general rule, mixes should be monitored at the kind of level at which they're eventually played by the listener.

air conditioning

The construction of professional studio air conditioning systems is beyond the scope of this book, and in any event it's impractical to fit these to a home studio because of the sheer volume of ducting, acoustic baffles and acoustically-isolated pumping machinery required. Professional systems such as these can be both hugely expensive and terribly bulky, and of course most need to be fitted while the studio is being constructed. Even so, some kind of ventilation is needed because a soundproof studio is also, by definition, effectively air tight. A few racks full of equipment generate a substantial amount of heat, and in a well-insulated room this means that cooling the air is actually a greater priority than piping in fresh air. In small studios, in which the doors can be opened for limited periods from time to time to ventilate the room, a heat-exchange air-cooling system may be quite adequate.

finding materials

Many of the materials used in sound isolation and acoustic treatment – such as mineral wool, plasterboard, flooring chipboard, roofing felt, insulation board and timber – can be found at a builders' merchant's yard. However, items such as barrier matting, half-round door gaskets, compression latches, specially-perforated peg boards, commercial floating flooring, neoprene and acoustic foam is less common, and has to be purchased from a specialist supplier of acoustic materials. Acoustic tiles are often offered for sale in the classified ads of most music magazines, although your local music store should also be able to order them for you. Other specialist companies may often be found in the *Yellow Pages*, the classified ads of music magazine or on the Internet.

common cable connections

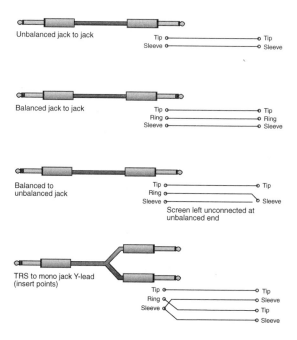

Unbalanced jack to jack

Tip o——————————o Tip
Sleeve o——————————o Sleeve

Balanced jack to jack

Tip o——————————o Tip
Ring o——————————o Ring
Sleeve o——————————o Sleeve

Balanced to
unbalanced jack

Tip o——————————o Tip
Ring o——
Sleeve o——————————o Sleeve

Screen left unconnected at
unbalanced end

TRS to mono jack Y-lead
(insert points)

Tip o——————————o Tip
Ring o——————————o Sleeve
Sleeve o——————————o Tip
——————————o Sleeve

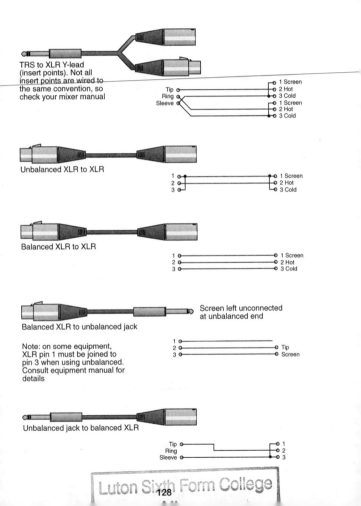

TRS to XLR Y-lead
(insert points). Not all
insert points are wired to
the same convention, so
check your mixer manual

Tip
Ring
Sleeve

1 Screen
2 Hot
3 Cold
1 Screen
2 Hot
3 Cold

Unbalanced XLR to XLR

1
2
3

1 Screen
2 Hot
3 Cold

Balanced XLR to XLR

1
2
3

1 Screen
2 Hot
3 Cold

Balanced XLR to unbalanced jack

Screen left unconnected
at unbalanced end

Note: on some equipment,
XLR pin 1 must be joined to
pin 3 when using unbalanced.
Consult equipment manual for
details

1
2
3

Tip
Screen

Unbalanced jack to balanced XLR

Tip
Ring
Sleeve

1
2
3

glossary

AC
Alternating Current.

active
Circuit containing transistors, ICs, tubes and other devices that require power to operate and are capable of amplification.

active sensing
System used to verify that a MIDI connection is working, in which the sending device frequently sends short messages to the receiving device to reassure it that all is well. If these active sensing messages stop for any reason, the receiving device will recognise a fault condition and switch off all notes. Not all MIDI devices support active sensing.

A/D converter
Circuit for converting analogue waveforms into a series of values represented by binary numbers. The more bits a converter has the greater the resolution of the sampling process. Current effects units are generally 16 bits or more, with the better models being either 20- or 24-bit.

ADSR
Envelope generator with Attack, Decay, Sustain and Release

parameters. This is a simple type of envelope generator and was first used on early analogue synthesisers, though similar envelopes may be found in some effects units to control filter sweeps and suchlike.

AFL

After-Fade Listen, a system used within mixing consoles to allow specific signals to be monitored at the level set by their fader or level control knob. Aux sends are generally monitored AFL rather than PFL so that the actual signal being fed to an effects unit can be monitored.

aftertouch

Means of generating a control signal based on how much pressure is applied to the keys of a MIDI keyboard. Most instruments that support this do not have independent pressure sensing for all keys but instead detect the overall pressure by means of a sensing strip running beneath the keys. Aftertouch may be used to control musical functions such as vibrato depth, filter brightness, loudness and so on, though it may also be used to control some parameter of a MIDI effects unit, such as delay feedback or effect level.

alpha version

Release version of software which may still contain some bugs (see Beta Version).

algorithm

Computer program designed to perform a specific task. In the context of effects units, algorithms usually describe a software building block designed to create a specific effect or combination of effects. All digital effects are based on algorithms.

aliasing

When an analogue signal is sampled for conversion into a digital data stream, the sampling frequency must be at least twice that of the highest frequency component of the input signal. If this rule is disobeyed, the sampling process becomes ambiguous, as there are insufficient points to define each waveform cycle, resulting in enharmonic sum and difference frequencies being added to the audible signal (see Nyquist Theorem).

ambience

The result of sound reflections in a confined space being added to the original sound. Ambience may also be created electronically by some digital reverb units. The main difference between ambience and reverberation is that ambience doesn't have the characteristic long delay time of reverberation – the reflections mainly give the sound a sense of space.

amp

Unit of electrical current, short for ampere.

amplifier

Device that increases the level of an electrical signal.

amplitude

Another word for level. Can refer to levels of sound or electrical signal.

analogue

Circuitry that uses a continually-changing voltage or current to represent a signal. The origin of the term is that the electrical signal can be thought of as being analogous to the original signal.

anti-aliasing filter
Filter used to limit the frequency range of an analogue signal prior to A/D conversion so that the maximum frequency does not exceed half the sampling rate.

application
Alternative term for computer program.

ASCII
American Standard Code for Information Interchange. A standard code for representing computer keyboard characters with binary data.

attack
Time taken for a sound to achieve maximum amplitude. Drums have a fast attack, whereas bowed strings have a slow attack. In compressors and gates, the attack time equates to how quickly the processor can change its gain.

attenuate
To make lower in level.

audio frequency
Signals in the human audio range, nominally 20Hz-20kHz.

aux
Control on a mixing console designed to route a proportion of the channel signal to the effects or cue mix outputs (see Aux Send).

aux return
Mixer inputs used to add effects to the mix.

aux send

Physical output from a mixer aux send buss.

backup

Safety copy of software or other digital data.

balance

This word has several meanings in recording. It may refer to the relative levels of the left and right channels of a stereo recording, or it may be used to describe the relative levels of the various instruments and voices within a mix.

balanced wiring

Wiring system which uses two out-of-phase conductors and a common screen to reduce the effect of interference. For balancing to be effective, both the sending and receiving device must have balanced output and input stages respectively.

bandpass filter (BDF)

Filter that removes or attenuates frequencies above and below the frequency at which it is set. Frequencies within the band are emphasised. Bandpass filters are often used in synthesisers as tone-shaping elements.

bandwidth

Means of specifying the range of frequencies passed by an electronic circuit such as an amplifier, mixer or filter. The frequency range is usually measured at the points where the level drops by 3dB relative to the maximum.

beta version

Version of software which is not fully tested and may still include bugs.

binary

Counting system based on only two numbers: one and zero.

bios

Part of a computer operating system held on ROM rather than on disk. This handles basic routines such as accessing the disk drive.

bit

Binary digit, which may either be one or zero.

boost/cut control

Single control which allows the range of frequencies passing through a filter to be either amplified or attenuated. The centre position is usually the 'flat' or 'no effect' position.

bouncing

Process of mixing two or more recorded tracks together and re-recording these onto another track.

BPM

Beats Per Minute.

breath controller

Device that converts breath pressure into MIDI controller data.

buffer

Circuit designed to isolate the output of a source device from loading effects due to the input impedance of the destination device.

buffer memory
Temporary RAM memory used in some computer operations, sometimes to prevent a break in the data stream when the computer is interrupted to perform another task.

bug
Slang term for software fault or equipment design problem.

buss
Common electrical signal path along which signals may travel. In a mixer, there are several busses carrying the stereo mix, the groups, the PFL signal, the aux sends and so on. Power supplies are also fed along busses.

byte
Piece of digital data comprising eight bits.

cardioid
Literally 'heart shaped'. Describes the polar response of a unidirectional microphone.

channel
In the context of MIDI, Channel refers to one of 16 possible data channels over which MIDI data may be sent. The organisation of data by channels means that up to 16 different MIDI instruments or parts may be addressed using a single cable.

channel
In the context of mixing consoles, a channel is a single strip of

controls relating to one input.

chase

Describes the process whereby a slave device attempts to synchronise itself with a master device. In the context of a MIDI sequence, Chase may also involve chasing events (looking back to earlier positions in the song to see if there are any program changes or other events that need to be acted upon).

chip

Integrated circuit.

chord

Two or more different musical notes played at the same time.

chorus

Effect created by doubling a signal and adding delay and pitch modulation.

chromatic

Describes a scale of pitches rising in steps of one semitone .

click track

Metronome pulse which helps musicians to keep time.

clipping

Severe form of distortion which occurs when a signal attempts to exceed the maximum level which a piece of equipment can handle.

clone

Exact duplicate. Often refers to digital copies of digital tapes.

common-mode rejection

Measure of how well a balanced circuit rejects a signal that is common to both inputs.

compander

Encode/decode device that compresses a signal while encoding it and then expands it when decoding it.

compressor

Device designed to reduce the dynamic range of audio signals by reducing the level of high signals or by increasing the level of low signals.

computer

Device for the storing and processing of digital data.

conductor

Material that provides a low resistance path for electrical current.

console

Alternative term for mixer.

contact enhancer

Compound designed to increase the electrical conductivity of electrical contacts such as plugs, sockets and edge connectors.

continuous controller

Type of MIDI message used to translate continuous change, such as from a pedal, wheel or breath control device.

copy protection

Method used by software manufacturers to prevent unauthorised copying.

crash
Slang term relating to malfunction of a computer program.

cut-and-paste editing
Copying or moving sections of a recording to different locations.

cutoff frequency
Frequency above or below which attenuation begins in a filter circuit.

cycle
One complete vibration of a sound source or its electrical equivalent. One cycle per second is expressed as one Hertz (Hz).

CV
Control Voltage. Used to control the pitch of an oscillator or filter frequency in an analogue synthesiser. Most analogue synthesisers follow a one volt per octave convention, though there are exceptions. To use a pre-MIDI analogue synthesiser under MIDI control, a MIDI-to-CV converter is required.

daisy chain
Term used to describe serial electrical connection between devices or modules.

damping
In the context of reverberation, damping refers to the rate at which reverberant energy is absorbed by the various surfaces in an environment.

DAT

Digital Audio Tape. The most commonly-used DAT machines are more correctly known as R-DATs because they use a rotating head similar to that in a video recorder. Digital recorders using fixed or stationary heads (such as DCC) are known as S-DAT machines.

data

Information stored and used by a computer.

data compression

System for reducing the amount of data stored by a digital system. Most audio data compression systems are known as lossy systems, as some of the original signal is discarded in accordance with psychoacoustic principles designed to ensure that only components which cannot be heard are lost.

dB

Decibel. Unit used to express the relative levels of two electrical voltages, powers or sounds.

dBm

Variation on dB referenced to 0dB = 1mW into 600ohms.

dBv

Variation on dB referenced to 0dB = 0.775v.

dBV

Variation on dB referenced to 0dB = 1V.

dB/octave

A means of measuring the slope of a filter. The more decibels per octave the sharper the filter slope.

dbx

A commercial encode/decode tape noise reduction system that compresses the signal during recording and expands it by an identical amount on playback.

DC

Direct Current.

DCC

Stationary-head digital recorder format developed by Philips. Uses a data-compression system to reduce the amount of data that needs to be stored.

DCO

Digitally-Controlled Oscillator.

DDL

Digital Delay Line.

decay

Progressive reduction in amplitude of a sound or electrical signal over time. In the context of an ADSR envelope shaper, the decay phase starts as soon as the attack phase has reached its maximum level. In the decay phase, the signal level drops until it reaches the sustain level set by the user. The signal then remains at this level until the key is released, at which point the release phase is entered.

de-esser

Device for reducing the effect of sibilance in vocal signals.

defragmentation

Process of rearranging the files on a hard disk so that all of the files are as contiguous as possible, and that the remaining free space is also contiguous.

deoxidising compound

Substance formulated to remove oxides from electrical contacts.

detent

Physical click stop in the centre of a control such as a pan or EQ cut/boost knob.

DI

Direct Inject, in which a signal is plugged directly into an audio chain without the aid of a microphone.

DI box

Device for matching the signal-level impedance of a source to a tape machine or mixer input.

digital

Electronic system which represents data and signals in the form of codes comprising ones and zeros.

digital delay

Digital processor for generating delay and echo effects.

digital reverb

Digital processor for simulating reverberation.

DIN connector

Consumer multipin signal connection format, also used for

MIDI cabling. Various pin configurations are available.

direct coupling

Means of connecting two electrical circuits so that both AC and DC signals may be passed between them.

disc

Used to describe vinyl discs, CDs and MiniDiscs.

disk

Abbreviation of diskette, but now used to describe computer floppy, hard and removable disks (see Floppy Disk).

dither

System of adding low-level noise to a digitised audio signal in a way which extends low-level resolution at the expense of a slight deterioration in noise performance.

DMA

Direct Memory Access. Part of a computer operating system that allows peripheral devices to communicate directly with the computer memory without going via the CPU (Central Processing Unit).

Dolby

An encode/decode tape noise reduction system that amplifies low-level, high-frequency signals during recording, then reverses this process during playback. There are several different Dolby systems in use, including types B, C and S for domestic and semi-professional machines, and types A and SR for professional machines. Recordings made whilst using one of these systems must also be replayed via the same system.

DOS

Disk Operating System. Part of the operating system of PC and PC-compatible computers.

driver

Piece of software that handles communications between the main program and a hardware peripheral, such as a soundcard, printer or scanner.

drum pad

Synthetic playing surface which produces electronic trigger signals in response to being hit with drumsticks.

dry

Signal to which no effects have been added. Conversely, a sound which has been treated with an effect, such as reverberation, is referred to as wet.

DSP

Digital Signal Processor. A powerful microchip used to process digital signals.

dubbing

Adding further material to an existing recording. Also known as overdubbing.

ducking

System for controlling the level of one audio signal with another. For example, background music can be made to duck whenever there is a voice-over.

dump

To transfer digital data from one device to another. A Sysex dump is a means of transmitting information about a particular instrument or module over MIDI, and may be used to store sound patches, parameter settings and so on.

dynamic microphone
Type of microphone that works on the electric generator principle, whereby a diaphragm moves a coil of wire within a magnetic field.

dynamic range
Range in decibels between the highest signal that can be handled by a piece of equipment and the level at which small signals disappear into the noise floor.

dynamics
Method of describing the relative levels within a piece of music.

early reflections
First sound reflections from walls, floors and ceilings following a sound which is created in an acoustically reflective environment.

effects loop
Connection system that allows an external signal processor to be connected into the audio chain.

effects return
Additional mixer input designed to accommodate the output from an effects unit.

effects unit

Device for treating an audio signal in order to change it in some creative way. Effects often involve the use of delay circuits, and include such treatments as reverb and echo.

encode/decode
System that requires a signal to be processed prior to recording, which is then reversed during playback.

enhancer
Device designed to brighten audio material using techniques such as dynamic equalisation, phase shifting and harmonic generation.

envelope
The way in which the level of a sound or signal varies over time.

envelope generator
Circuit capable of generating a control signal which represents the envelope of the sound you want to recreate. This may then be used to control the level of an oscillator or other sound source, though envelopes may also be used to control filter or modulation settings. The most common example is the ADSR generator.

E-PROM
Similar to ROM, but the information on the chip can be erased and replaced using special equipment.

equaliser
Device for selectively cutting or boosting selected parts of the audio spectrum.

erase
To remove recorded material from an analogue tape, or to remove digital data from any form of storage medium.

event
In MIDI terms, an event is a single unit of MIDI data, such as a note being turned on or off, a piece of controller information, a program change, and so on.

exciter
Enhancer that works by synthesising new high-frequency harmonics.

expander
Device designed to decrease the level of low-level signals and increase the level of high-level signals, thus increasing the dynamic range of the signal.

expander module
Synthesiser with no keyboard, often rack mountable or in some other compact format.

fader
Sliding potentiometer used in mixers and other processors.

FET
Field Effect Transistor.

figure-of-eight
Describes the polar response of a microphone that is equally sensitive at both front and rear, yet rejects sounds coming from the sides.

file

Meaningful list of data stored in digitally. A Standard MIDI File is a specific type of file designed to allow sequence information to be exchanged between different types of sequencer.

filter

Electronic circuit designed to emphasise or attenuate a specific range of frequencies.

flanging

Modulated delay effect using feedback to create a dramatic, sweeping sound.

floppy disk

Computer disk that uses a flexible magnetic medium encased in a protective plastic sleeve. The maximum capacity of a standard high-density disk is 1.44Mb. Earlier double-density disks hold only around half that amount of data.

flutter echo

Resonant echo that occurs when sound reflects back and forth between two parallel reflective surfaces.

foldback

System for feeding one or more separate mixes to the performers for use while recording and overdubbing. Also known as a cue mix.

formant

Frequency component or resonance of an instrument or voice sound that doesn't change with the pitch of the note being played or sung. For example, the body resonance of an acoustic guitar remains constant regardless of the note being played.

format
Procedure required to ready a computer disk for use. Formatting organises the disk's surface into a series of electronic pigeonholes into which data can be stored. Different computers often use different formatting systems.

fragmentation
Process by which the available space on a disk drive is split up into small sections due to the storing and erasing of files (see Defragmentation).

frequency
Indication of how many cycles of a repetitive waveform occur in one second. A waveform which has a repetition cycle of once per second has a frequency of 1Hz.

frequency response
Measurement of the frequency range that can be handled by a specific piece of electrical equipment or loudspeaker.

FSK
Frequency-Shift Keying. A method of recording a sync clock signal onto tape by representing it as two alternating tones.

fundamental
Any sound comprises a fundamental or basic frequency plus harmonics and partials at a higher frequency.

FX

Shorthand for effects.

gain
Amount by which a circuit amplifies a signal.

gate
Electrical signal that is generated whenever a key is depressed on an electronic keyboard. This is used to trigger envelope generators and other events that need to be synchronised to key action.

gate
Electronic device designed to mute low-level signals, thus improving the noise performance during pauses in the wanted material.

general MIDI
Addition to the basic MIDI spec to assure a minimum level of compatibility when playing back GM-format song files. The specification covers type and program, number of sounds, minimum levels of polyphony and multitimbrality, response to controller information and so on.

glitch
Describes an unwanted short-term corruption of a signal, or the unexplained short-term malfunction of a piece of equipment. For example, an inexplicable click on a DAT tape would be termed a glitch.

GM reset
Universal Sysex command which activates the General MIDI mode on a GM instrument. The same command also sets all

controllers to their default values and switches off any notes still playing by means of an All Notes Off message.

graphic equaliser

Equaliser on which several narrow segments of the audio spectrum are controlled by individual cut/boost faders. The name derives from the fact that the fader positions provide a graphic representation of the EQ curve.

ground

Electrical earth, or zero volts. In mains wiring, the ground cable is physically connected to the ground via a long conductive metal spike.

ground loops

Also known as earth loops. Wiring problem in which currents circulate in the ground wiring of an audio system, known as the ground loop effect. When these currents are induced by the alternating mains supply, hum results.

group

Collection of signals within a mixer that are mixed and then routed through a separate fader to provide overall control. In a multitrack mixer, several groups are provided to feed the various recorder track inputs.

GS

Roland's own extension to the General MIDI protocol.

hard disk

High-capacity computer storage device based on a rotating rigid disk with a magnetic coating onto which data may be recorded.

harmonic

High-frequency component of a complex waveform.

harmonic distortion

Addition of harmonics not previously present in the original signal.

head

Part of a tape machine or disk drive that reads and/or writes data to and from the storage media.

headroom

The safety margin in decibels between the highest peak signal being passed by a piece of equipment and the absolute maximum level the equipment can handle.

high-pass filter (HPF)

Filter which attenuates frequencies below its cutoff frequency.

hiss

Noise caused by random electrical fluctuations.

hum

Signal contamination caused by the addition of low frequencies, usually related to the mains power frequency.

Hz

Shorthand for Hertz, the unit of frequency.

IC

Integrated Circuit.

impedance

Can be visualised as the AC resistance of a circuit which contains both resistive and reactive components.

inductor

Reactive component which presents an impedance with increases with frequency.

initialise

To automatically restore a piece of equipment to its factory default settings.

insert point

Connector that allows an external processor to be patched into a signal path so that the signal then flows through the external processor.

insulator

Material that does not conduct electricity.

interface

Device that acts as an intermediary to two or more other pieces of equipment. For example, a MIDI interface enables a computer to communicate with MIDI instruments and keyboards.

intermittent

Usually describes a fault that only appears occasionally.

intermodulation distortion

Form of distortion that introduces frequencies not present in the original signal. These are invariably based on the sum and difference products of the original frequencies.

I/O

The part of a system that handles inputs and outputs, usually in the digital domain.

IPS

Inches Per Second. Used to describe tape speed.

IRQ

Interrupt Request. Part of the operating system of a computer that allows a connected device to request attention from the processor in order to transfer data to it or from it.

isopropyl alcohol

Type of alcohol commonly used for cleaning and de-greasing tape machine heads and guides.

jack

Commonly used audio connector. May be mono (TS) or stereo (TRS).

jargon

Specialised words associated with a specialist subject.

k

Abbreviation for 1000 (kilo). Used as a prefix to other values to indicate magnitude.

kHz

1000Hz.

kohm

1000 ohms.

LCD
Liquid Crystal Display.

LED
Light-Emitting Diode. Solid-state lamp.

LSB
Least Significant Byte. If a piece of data has to be conveyed as two bytes, one byte represents high-value numbers and the other low-value numbers, in much the same way as tens and units function in the decimal system. The high value, or most significant part of the message, is called the Most Significant Byte or MSB.

limiter
Device that controls the gain of a signal so as to prevent it from ever exceeding a preset level. A limiter is essentially a fast-acting compressor with an infinite compression ratio.

linear
Device where the output is a direct multiple of the input.

line level
Mixers and signal processors tend to work at a standard signal level known as line level. In practice there are several different standard line levels, but all are in the order of a few volts. A nominal signal level is around -10dBv for semi-pro equipment and +4dBv for professional equipment.

load
Electrical circuit that draws power from another circuit or power supply. Also describes reading data into a computer.

load on/off
Function to allow the keyboard and sound-generating section of a keyboard synthesiser to be used independently of each other.

logic
Type of electronic circuitry used for processing binary signals comprising two discrete voltage levels.

loop
Circuit where the output is connected back to the input.

low-frequency oscillator (LFO)
Oscillator used as a modulation source, usually below 20Hz. The most common LFO waveshape is the sine wave, though there is often a choice of sine, square, triangular and sawtooth waveforms.

low-pass filter (LPF)
A filter which attenuates frequencies above its cutoff frequency.

mA
Milliamp, or one thousandth of an amp.

MDM
Modular Digital Multitrack. A digital recorder that can be used in multiples to provide a greater number of synchronised tracks than a single machine.

meg
Abbreviation for 1,000,000.

memory
Computer's RAM memory used to store programs and data. This data is lost when the computer is switched off and so must be stored to disk or other suitable media.

menu
List of choices presented by a computer program or a device with a display window.

mic level
Low-level signal generated by a microphone. This must be amplified many times to increase it to line level.

microprocessor
Specialised microchip at the heart of a computer. It is here that instructions are read and acted upon.

MIDI
Musical Instrument Digital Interface.

MIDI analyser
Device that gives a visual readout of MIDI activity when connected between two pieces of MIDI equipment.

MIDI bank change
Type of controller message used to select alternate banks of MIDI programs where access to more than 128 programs is required.

MIDI controller
Term used to describe the physical interface by means of which the musician plays the MIDI synthesiser or other sound

generator. Examples of controllers are keyboards, drum pads, wind synths and so on.

MIDI control change
Also known as MIDI Controllers or Controller Data. These messages convey positional information relating to performance controls such as wheels, pedals, switches and other devices. This information can be used to control functions such as vibrato depth, brightness, portamento, effects levels, and many other parameters.

(standard) MIDI file
Standard file format for storing song data recorded on a MIDI sequencer in such as way as to allow it to be read by other makes or models of MIDI sequencer.

MIDI implementation chart
A chart, usually found in MIDI product manuals, which provides information as to which MIDI features are supported. Supported features are marked with a 0 while unsupported feature are marked with a X. Additional information may be provided, such as the exact form of the bank change message.

MIDI in
The socket used to receive information from a master controller or from the MIDI Thru socket of a slave unit.

MIDI merge
Device or sequencer function that enables two or more streams of MIDI data to be combined.

MIDI mode

MIDI information can be interpreted by the receiving MIDI instrument in a number of ways, the most common being polyphonically on a single MIDI channel (poly-omni off mode). Omni mode enables a MIDI Instrument to play all incoming data regardless of channel.

MIDI module
Sound-generating device with no integral keyboard.

MIDI note number
Every key on a MIDI keyboard has its own note number, ranging from 0 to 127, where 60 represents middle C. Some systems use C3 as middle C while others use C4.

MIDI note off
MIDI message sent when key is released.

MIDI note on
Message sent when note is pressed.

MIDI out
MIDI connector used to send data from a master device to the MIDI In of a connected slave device.

MIDI port
MIDI connections of a MIDI-compatible device. A multiport, in the context of a MIDI interface, is a device with multiple MIDI output sockets, each capable of carrying data relating to a different set of 16 MIDI channels. Multiports are the only means of exceeding the limitations imposed by 16 MIDI channels.

MIDI program change

Type of MIDI message used to change sound patches on a remote module or the effects patch on a MIDI effects unit.

MIDI splitter
Alternative term for MIDI thru box.

MIDI sync
Description of the synchronisation systems available to MIDI users: MIDI Clock and MIDI Time Code.

MIDI thru
Socket on a slave unit used to feed the MIDI In socket of the next unit in line.

MIDI thru box
Device which splits the MIDI Out signal of a master instrument or sequencer to avoid daisy chaining. Powered circuitry is used to 'buffer' the outputs so as to prevent problems when many pieces of equipment are driven from a single MIDI output.

mixer
Device for combining two or more audio signals.

monitor
Reference loudspeaker used for mixing.

monitor
VDU for a computer.

monitoring
Action of listening to a mix or a specific audio signal.

monophonic
One note at a time.

motherboard
Main circuit board within a computer into which all the other components plug or connect.

MTC
MIDI Time Code. A MIDI sync implementation based on SMPTE time code.

multisample
Creation of several samples, each covering a limited musical range, the idea being to produce a more natural range of sounds across the range of the instrument being sampled. For example, a piano may need to be sampled every two or three semitones in order to sound convincing.

multitimbral module
MIDI sound source capable of producing several different sounds at the same time and controlled on different MIDI channels.

multitrack
Recording device capable of recording several 'parallel' parts or tracks which may then be mixed or re-recorded independently.

near field
Some people prefer the term 'close field' to describe a loudspeaker system designed to be used close to the listener. The advantage is that the listener hears more of the direct

sound from the speakers and less of the reflected sound from the room.

noise reduction
System for reducing analogue tape noise or for reducing the level of hiss present in a recording.

noise shaping
System for creating digital dither so that any added noise is shifted into those parts of the audio spectrum where the human ear is least sensitive.

non-linear recording
Describes digital recording systems that allow any parts of the recording to be played back in any order with no gaps. Conventional tape is referred to as linear, because the material can only play back in the order in which it was recorded.

non-registered parameter number
Addition to the basic MIDI spec that allows controllers 98 and 99 to be used to control non-standard parameters relating to particular models of synthesiser. This is an alternative to using system-exclusive data to achieve the same ends, though NRPNs tend to be used mainly by Yamaha and Roland instruments.

normalise
A socket is said to be normalised when it is wired such that the original signal path is maintained, unless a plug is inserted into the socket. The most common examples of normalised connectors are the insert points on a mixing console.

nut

Slotted plastic or bone component at the headstock end of a guitar neck used to guide the strings over the fingerboard, and to space the strings above the frets.

Nyquist theorem

The rule which states that a digital sampling system must have a sample rate at least twice as high as that of the highest frequency being sampled in order to avoid aliasing. Because anti-aliasing filters aren't perfect, the sampling frequency usually has to be made more than twice that of the maximum input frequency.

octave

When a frequency or pitch is transposed up by one octave, its frequency is doubled.

off-line

Process carried out while a recording is not playing. For example, some computer-based processes have to be carried out off-line as the computer isn't fast enough to carry out the process in real time.

ohm

Unit of electrical resistance.

omni

Refers to a microphone that is equally sensitive in all directions, or to the MIDI mode in which data on all channels is recognised.

open circuit

Break in an electrical circuit that prevents current from flowing.

open reel

Tape machine on which the tape is wound on spools rather than sealed in a cassette.

operating system

Basic software that enables a computer to load and run other programs.

opto-electronic device

Device on which some electrical parameters change in response to a variation in light intensity. Variable photoresistors are sometimes used as gain control elements in compressors where the side-chain signal modulates the light intensity.

oscillator

Circuit designed to generate a periodic electrical waveform.

overdub

To add another part to a multitrack recording or to replace one of the existing parts (see Dubbing).

overload

To exceed the operating capacity of an electronic or electrical circuit.

pad

Resistive circuit for reducing signal level.

pan pot

Control enabling the user of a mixer to move the signal to any point in the stereo soundstage by varying the relative levels fed to the left and right stereo outputs.

parallel

Method of connecting two or more circuits together so that their inputs and outputs are all connected together.

parameter

Variable value that affects some aspect of a device's performance.

parametric EQ

Equaliser with separate controls for frequency, bandwidth and cut/boost.

passive

Circuit with no active elements.

patch

Alternative term for program. Referring to a single programmed sound within a synthesiser that can be called up using program-change commands. MIDI effects units and samplers also have patches.

patch bay

System of panel-mounted connectors used to bring inputs and outputs to a central point from where they can be routed using plug-in patch cords.

patch cord

Short cable used with patch bays.

peak

Maximum instantaneous level of a signal.

peak

The highest signal level in any section of programme material.

PFL

Pre-Fade Listen. A system used within a mixing console to allow the operator to listen in on a selected signal, regardless of the position of the fader controlling that signal.

phantom power

48V DC supply for capacitor microphones, transmitted along the signal cores of a balanced mic cable.

phase

Timing difference between two electrical waveforms expressed in degrees where 360° corresponds to a delay of exactly one cycle.

phaser

Effect which combines a signal with a phase-shifted version of itself to produce creative filtering effects. Most phasers are controlled by means of an LFO.

phono plug

Hi-fi connector developed by RCA and used extensively on semi-pro, unbalanced recording equipment.

pickup

Part of a guitar that converts string vibrations to electrical signals.

pitch

Musical interpretation of an audio frequency.

pitch bend

Special control message specifically designed to produce a change in pitch in response to the movement of a pitch bend wheel or lever. Pitch bend data can be recorded and edited, just like any other MIDI controller data, even though it isn't part of the controller message group.

pitch shifter

Device for changing the pitch of an audio signal without changing its duration.

polyphony

An instrument's ability to play two or more notes simultaneously. An instrument which can play only one note at a time is described as monophonic.

poly mode

The most common MIDI mode, which allows any instrument to respond to multiple simultaneous notes transmitted on a single MIDI channel.

port

Connection for the input or output of data.

portamento

Gliding effect that allows a sound to change pitch gradually when a new key is pressed or MIDI note sent.

post-production

Work done to a stereo recording after mixing is complete.

post-fade

Aux signal taken from after the channel fader so that the aux send level follows any channel fader changes. Normally used for feeding effects devices.

power supply

Unit designed to convert mains electricity to the voltages necessary to power an electronic circuit or device.

PPM

Peak Programme Meter. A meter designed to register signal peaks rather than the average level.

PPQN

Pulsed Per Quarter Note. Used in the context of MIDI clock-derived sync signals.

pre-emphasis

System for applying high-frequency boost to a sound before processing so as to reduce the effect of noise. A corresponding de-emphasis process is required on playback so as to restore the original signal and to attenuate any high-frequency noise contributed by the recording process.

pre-fade

Aux signal taken from before the channel fader so that the channel fader has no effect on the aux send level. Normally used for creating foldback or cue mixes.

preset

Effects unit or synth patch that cannot be altered by the user.

pressure

Alternative term for aftertouch.

processor

Device designed to treat an audio signal by changing its dynamics or frequency content. Examples of processors include compressors, gates and equalisers.

pulse-width modulation

Means of modulating the duty cycle (mark/space ratio) of a pulse wave. This changes the timbre of the basic tone. LFO modulation of pulse width can be used to produce a pseudo-chorus effect.

punch-in

Action of placing an already recorded track into record at the correct time during playback so that the existing material may be extended or replaced.

punch-out

Action of switching a tape machine (or other recording device) out of record after executing a punch in. With most multitrack machines, both punching in and punching out can be accomplished without stopping the tape.

PZM

Pressure Zone Microphone. A type of boundary microphone, designed to reject out-of-phase sounds reflected from surfaces within the recording environment.

Q

Measurement of the resonant properties of a filter. The higher the Q, the more resonant the filter and the narrower the range of frequencies that are allowed to pass.

quantising

Means of moving notes recorded in a MIDI sequencer so that they line up with user defined subdivisions of a musical bar – 16s, for example. The facility may be used to correct timing errors, but over-quantising can remove the human feel from a performance.

R-DAT

Digital tape machine using a rotating head system.

real time

Audio process that can be carried out as the signal is being recorded or played back. The opposite is off-line, where the signal is processed in non-real time.

release

Time taken for a level or gain to return to normal. Often used to describe the rate at which a synthesised sound reduces in level after a key has been released.

resistance

Opposition to the flow of electrical current. Measured in ohms.

resolution

Accuracy with which an analogue signal is represented by a digitising system. The more bits are used, the more accurately the amplitude of each sample can be measured, but there are other elements of converter design that also affect accuracy. High conversion accuracy is known as high resolution.

resonance
Same as Q.

reverb
Acoustic ambience created by multiple reflections in a confined space.

RF
Radio Frequency.

RF interference
Interference which takes place significantly above the range of human hearing.

ribbon microphone
Microphone in which the sound-capturing element is a thin metal ribbon suspended in a magnetic filed. When sound causes the ribbon to vibrate, a small electrical current is generated within the ribbon.

roll-off
The rate at which a filter attenuates a signal once it has passed the filter cutoff point.

safety copy
Copy or clone of an original tape for use in case of loss of or damage to the original.

sample
Process carried out by an A/D converter where the instantaneous amplitude of a signal is measured many times per second (44.1kHz in the case of CD).

sample

Digitised sound used as a musical sound source in a sampler or additive synthesiser.

sample rate

Number of times which an A/D converter samples the incoming waveform each second.

SCSI

(Pronounced 'skuzzi'.) Small Computer System Interface. An interfacing system for using hard drives, scanners, CD-ROM drives and similar peripherals with a computer. Each SCSI device has its own ID number and no two SCSI devices in the same chain must be set to the same number. The last SCSI device in the chain should be terminated either via an internal terminator, where provided, or via a plug-in terminator fitted to a free SCSI socket.

sequencer

Device for recording and replaying MIDI data, usually in a multitrack format, allowing complex compositions to be built up a part at a time.

sibilance

High-frequency whistling or lisping sound that affects vocal recordings due either to poor mic technique or excessive equalisation.

side chain

Part of a circuit that splits off a proportion of the main signal to be processed in some way. Compressors use a side-chain signal to derive their control signals.

signal
Electrical representation of input such as sound.

signal chain
Route taken by a signal from the input of a system to its output.

signal-to-noise ratio
Ratio of maximum signal level to the residual noise, expressed in decibels.

SPL
Sound-Pressure Level. Measured in decibels.

stereo
Two-channel system feeding left and right loudspeakers.

surge
Sudden increase in mains voltage.

sustain
Part of the ADSR envelope which determines the level to which the sound will settle if a key is held down. Once the key is released, the sound decays at a rate set by the release parameter. Also refers to a guitar's ability to hold notes which decay very slowly.

sweet spot
Optimum position for a microphone or a listener relative to monitor loudspeakers.

sync
System for making two or more pieces of equipment run in

synchronism with each other.

synthesiser
Electronic musical instrument designed to create a wide range of sounds, both imitative and abstract.

tape head
Part of a tape machine that transfers magnetic energy to the tape during recording or reads it during playback.

tempo
Rate of the beat of a piece of music, measured here in beats per minute.

track
This term dates back to multitrack tape, on which the tracks are physical stripes of recorded material located side by side along the length of the tape.

transpose
To shift a musical signal by a fixed number of semitones.

tremolo
Modulation of the amplitude of a sound using an LFO.

TRS jack
Stereo-type jack with tip, ring and sleeve connections.

unbalanced
Two-wire electrical signal connection where the inner (or hot, or positive) conductor is usually surrounded by the outer (or cold, or negative) conductor, forming a screen against interference.

unison
To play the same melody using two or more different instruments or voices.

valve
~~Vacuum-tube amplification component, also known as a tube.~~

vibrato
Pitch modulation using an LFO to modulate a VCO.

voice
Capacity of a synthesiser to play a single musical note. An instrument capable of playing 16 simultaneous notes is said to be a 16-voice instrument.

volt
Unit of electrical power.

VU meter
Meter designed to interpret signal levels in roughly the same way as the human ear, which responds more closely to the average levels of sounds rather than to the peak levels.

warmth
Subjective term used to describe sound where the bass and low mid frequencies have depth and where the high frequencies are smooth sounding rather than being aggressive or fatiguing. Warm-sounding tube equipment may also exhibit some of the aspects of compression.

watt
Unit of electrical power.

waveform

Graphic representation of the way in which a sound wave or electrical wave varies with time.

white noise

Random signal with an energy distribution that produces the same amount of noise power per Hz.

write

To save data to a digital storage medium, such as a hard drive.

XG

Yamaha's alternative to Roland's GS system for enhancing the General MIDI protocol so as to provide additional banks of patches and further editing facilities.

XLR

Type of connector commonly used to carry balanced audio signals, including the feeds from microphones.

Y-lead

Lead split so that one source can feed two destinations. Y-leads may also be used in console insert points, when a stereo jack plug at one end of the lead is split into two monos at the other.

zero crossing point

Point at which a signal waveform crosses from being positive to negative and vice versa.

zipper noise

Audible steps that occur when a parameter is being varied in a digital audio processor.